Practica

Practical Bee-keeping

Herbert Mace

Edited in consultation with Karl Showler

Ward Lock Limited·London

Acknowledgements

The publishers would like to thank J. Spiller and
M. G. Apiaries for permission to reproduce
several line drawings; Mr Graham Burtt for the
loan of blocks of appliances; Eric Greenwood
and Karl Showler for their kind help in
supplying photographs.

ISBN 0 7063 6420 1

This edition first published in Great Britain in 1977
by Ward Lock Limited, 82 Gower Street,
London, WC1E 6EQ, an Egmont Company.
Reprinted 1985.

House editor E. M. Cadell

Layout by Heather Sherratt

Front cover photograph by John Mason, Ardea London
Back cover photograph by Ian Beams, Ardea London

Text filmset in Times Roman (327)

Printed and bound in Great Britain by
Hollen Street Press Ltd, Slough, Berkshire

Contents

Introduction

Bee-keeping is one of the most ancient crafts known to man, evolving naturally from the original skills of those who gathered honey from the wild. The Roman era brought widespread use of wicker and clay hives, and these continued to be used up to the time of the Industrial Revolution in Britain. At that time cheap imported sugar and refined mineral oils threatened the production of honey and wax. However, in the closing decades of the nineteenth century a number of fundamental technical advances were made, which moved bee-keeping from a mystery of fixed-comb skeps to the easily opened movable-comb hives of today: the metal smoker permitted the subjugation of the colony of bees; the extractor allowed for the production of liquid honey without destruction of the combs; and the mass-produced cheap glass jar provided efficient storage for marketing.

In recent years bee-keeping has entered upon a remarkable period of expansion. Associations of bee-keepers report large numbers of new members. Their lecture programmes are planned to assist the beginner, and many provide classes in all aspects of bee-keeping, from hive construction to analysis of the pollen spectrum of honey.

This book has been based on Herbert Mace's *The Complete Handbook of Bee-keeping*, which has been printed in several editions, the first of which appeared in 1952. This compact version is intended to act as an introduction to the basic techniques and skills of bee-keeping for the beginner, and the material extracted from *The Complete Handbook* has been selected with that aim in view.

Much of the appeal of bee-keeping lies in its combination of the simple rural pursuit with the sophistication of the latest in applied science. Some bee-keepers conduct their bee-keeping on strictly economic lines, and look for a financial return on their labours; others see what they do purely as a hobby, and spend more on their bees than they could hope to recoup financially. All will agree that bees and bee-keeping are a source of endless fascination, and I hope that this book will prove both a tribute to a great bee-keeper and an introduction to an ancient but very active craft.

Karl Showler

1 Choosing a Hive

There are several ways of making a start in bee-keeping. Those who already know something of the subject, or have bee-keeping neighbours, frequently begin with a swarm, often presented free at the end of the season, or even found at large. Those who start without such advantages should study the subject well and master the main principles in theory. Then, having obtained the hive and the essential tools described, a colony of bees on six to ten combs can be bought about April. Although this will mean the largest cash outlay, it is the most promising investment, for if the season proves a good one there may be a good crop of honey, perhaps enough to pay for the whole outlay. Such a colony is complete with queen, workers, comb, honey and brood. A few minutes spent in examining it will teach the novice more than a great deal of reading.

In the natural way, bees attach the comb to the walls of a cavity wherever it may be, and if we are content to have fixed comb hives, it follows that any kind of waterproof box or basket will serve as a beehive. However well this may suit the bees, it is very inconvenient for the bee-keeper and the advantages of movable combs are so great that it is now considered essential for each to be enclosed in a frame.

Frames

The only satisfactory shape for a frame is rectangular; others have been tried, but without success. All must be the same size, and the standard plan is to make them with projecting ends or 'lugs', which rest on a ledge inside the walls of the hive. Amateur hive makers are apt to go sadly wrong in the matter of bee-space, either by making the hive only just large enough to take the frames, or, on the other hand, leaving as much as an inch (2·5 cm) of space each side of the frame. Since the bees either seal them in or brace them together, the frames can only be removed by force, and this often causes serious damage to the comb and bees. So long as the space on either side of the frame is between $\frac{3}{16}$ and $\frac{5}{16}$ in (4·8–8 mm), it will be left open as a passageway.

The next point to consider is the best number of frames to make up a brood-chamber. For many years ten were considered adequate, but it is now recognized that swarming is best controlled by giving ample space. Larger colonies are given more room by adding another similar box above, which provides the queen with a run of twenty combs. A modification of this is to use a shallow frame box, as usually employed for surplus honey, so that the queen can extend her brood into it if necessary.

Wax foundation   Frames are of no use without wax foundation, because it is the presence of this wax in the frame which ensures that

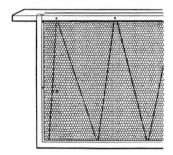

Frame with Lee's wired foundation

the bees will build *inside* the frame. Foundation is sold in the correct size for each type of frame and is available with or without strengthening wires, since some people prefer to insert the wire themselves.

Hives

Five distinct types of hives are in general use today and it will be sufficient introduction to the subject if I describe and illustrate them.

W.B.C. hive   Named after its inventor, W. B. Carr, this hive became widely popular, having at one time been strongly recommended by the British Bee-keepers' Association.

It has the floor on legs, light inner brood-chamber and outer cases, which leave a space of 2 in (5 cm) or more round the brood-box, and permit shallow frame racks, standard brood-chambers or section racks to be added, either above or below the brood-nest.

A considerable drawback is the large number of separate parts which make up this hive, so that the outer cases have to be removed

W.B.C. brood-chamber

before the inner parts are reached. The hive has many varieties, the best being that in which the outer cases are square and overlap each other. The worst are those which *look* square but are, in fact, an inch (2·5 cm) or so larger one way, and these should be avoided. The square form holds ten frames, but some patterns take twelve or more. The British Standards Institution specification 1300/1946 is now superseding other forms of W.B.C.

Apart from the extra trouble of manipulating, the W.B.C. is a good, serviceable hive, with the advantage that the inner boxes are light, portable and cheap. Perhaps its chief merit is that it is easier to keep the brood-chamber dry in winter than in other forms.

National hive This is now the commonest type of single-walled hive in use in the U.K. Its chief merit is that each storey is complete in one square unit, which can be used in any position on any hive of its kind. The roof is flat, covered with zinc or felt, and seldom blows off. Eleven frames are contained in the brood-chamber. Perhaps its weak point is the floor, which slopes gently from the back to the end of the alighting board. It does not throw rain off fast enough and damp may seep back into the hive. In some models none of the floor projects in front, so that rain has no lodging place, and the hive is easier to transport on a vehicle. No legs are fitted to this hive, which should stand on bricks or a wooden stage.

Smith hive A hive commonly used in Scotland known as the Smith, after its maker, is a modification of the National, using British Standard frames, but with shortened lugs as in the American forms. It is correspondingly cheap and has the advantage that those at present using any form of hive with B.S. combs can adopt it without sacrificing any equipment, all that is necessary being to cut down the lugs to the $\frac{9}{16}$ in (14·3 mm) length.

9

Langstroth and Modified Dadant hives   The Langstroth and Modified Dadant hives are single-walled hives of American origin, constructed on lines similar to the Smith hive but with larger dimensions.

All the English-speaking countries of the world use the Langstroth as their standard hive, though it is not so widely used in Europe and the United Kingdom.

Langstroth hive with entrance ramp; its crownboard is fitted with a large perspex window

Observation hives   Those whose interest in bees makes them wish to study them intimately can obtain a specially designed hive that enables every detail of the interior to be inspected. Although unsuitable as a permanent home, this hive can be furnished with a small colony in the spring and maintained all summer, during which time every phase of hive life can be witnessed.

All observation hives are made so that a comb is accommodated between glass sides. It may hold only one comb, or two or more, one above another. To ensure retention of heat, the glass sides are provided with wooden or cloth covers. The hive can stand in any room, and communicates with the open air through a tunnel leading from the bottom.

Materials and finish for hives   The material of which hives are made must be sound and well seasoned. Lightness is also an advantage. Yellow deal was for a long time considered best, but Canadian Red Cedar has become popular. It is light, durable and needs no treatment to preserve it from weather, which merely turns it to a pleasing grey shade. If other woods are used, some form of treatment will be needed. At one time lead paint was always used, partly because it is

10

the standard preservative for wood and partly because the colour of the hive has some bearing on the bees' welfare. White paint is a general favourite, but has the drawback of looking shabby very quickly. The other chief favourites are pale blue and stone colour, though green is sometimes chosen. Double-walled hives like the W.B.C. are best painted, but for single-walled ones creosote or other insecticide-free preservative is admirable, for it gives protection from rain, while permitting internal moisture to escape, and is quickly applied.

Of recent years, especially since timber became so dear, other materials have been tried for hives. Plastics are being used, but are expensive and only in the experimental stage.

Plans for making your own hive are obtainable from the British Bee-keepers' Association.

Spacing   In all hives the frames hang parallel with each other and the distance from centre to centre is $1\frac{9}{20}$ in (37 mm), so that when the comb is built out there will be an exact bee-space between combs and no room for other comb. Proper spacing is secured by various devices, of which the most usual in Britain are the 'W.B.C. metal ends', which slide onto the lug. These do have drawbacks, the worst being that when combs are put into the honey extractor, they are apt to catch in the metal-work, so that they should be removed and replaced afterwards. Short lug frames have no room for metal ends and, in the U.S., spacing is by the Hoffman frame, in which the side bars have their upper third widened so that they are automatically spaced when brought together. In addition to the frames, room is allowed in the brood-chamber for a division board. It is not essential, but it is useful when the chamber is very full, for it can be removed easily to allow room for the frames to be separated. It can also be employed to reduce the area of a brood-chamber when only a few combs are occupied by bees.

Covering the frames   To complete the hive the frames must be covered with something readily removable, made of any suitable material—thin board, or composition board. If the hive is made with a bee-space between the frame tops and the top of the wall, the cover can be laid over as it is, but when the frames are flush with the hive top, a $\frac{1}{4}$ in (6 mm) thick rim is fixed round the board so that only the hive wall comes in contact with it. In either case, this leaves a bee-space over the frames, which are kept clean, and room is allowed for bees to pass freely over them—a great advantage in winter. The board is easily removed by inserting the hive tool under one corner. The addition of two holes to take Porter bee escapes converts the cover board into a clearer board; when not in use, they can be covered by a piece of glass or perforated zinc.

Supers

In addition to the parts already described, supers for surplus honey are needed. They are of two kinds, one for the storage of honey for extracting, the other for sections. The former are made in the same manner as the brood-chamber, the size varying with the type of hive. Most people use a shallow frame super, which holds frames $5\frac{1}{2}$ in (14 cm) deep, but many think it a mistake to have two kinds of frame and use brood-chambers as supers. In W.B.C. hives each super must have a 'lift' or outer case to correspond. The minimum requirement is two supers per hive. In a good season, three, four or even more may be required, but in practice, when there are several hives, there are usually some which do not need more than one, leaving spares for the more advanced colonies.

The rack for sections is a bottomless box, fitted with bars beneath to support the sections, the number of which varies with the size of the brood-chamber. In the W.B.C. there are twenty-one in rows of three; in the National thirty-two in rows of four.

The excluder

A matter on which there has always been sharp division of opinion is the use of 'excluder'. This is a metal screen covering the top of the brood-chamber. It may be made of stiff wire or sheet zinc closely perforated with slots, through which workers bees can just squeeze but too small for the queen to negotiate.

Wire queen excluder

Some will have nothing to do with queen excluder. They contend that the queen should not be hampered in any way, because the more brood there is, the stronger the colony will become and the more honey it will store. Those who favour excluders complain that not only is brood mixed up with honey if the queen goes into the supers, but that much pollen is also stored there.

Hive stands

Hives with legs can stand on a concrete platform, or a brick or slate should be put underneath each leg, or it will soon rot. National hives can be supported on bricks or wooden joists on stands made of 2×2 in (5×5 cm) timber, joined together by cross-pieces at the ends. These are laid down on bricks and are long enough to take two hives. This is a very convenient arrangement, for some of the best swarm-control methods and those connected with queen rearing make it necessary for two hives to stand side by side for a certain time. Not more than two should be on a stand, so that each hive can be manipulated from the back or side.

If hives are kept in a low-lying spot, it is important to make certain that they cannot be flooded. Stands of sufficient height to keep the hives above maximum flood level must be erected and securely embedded, so that they cannot be washed away.

2 Bee-keeping Equipment

Tools and equipment

Smoker The most ancient of the bee-keeper's tools is the smoker. Originally nothing more than a piece of smouldering wood or fabric, the modern article consists of a fire-box connected with a bellows operated with one hand. It is easily supplied with fresh fuel and will burn for hours when properly charged. Cartridges of corrugated paper, old rags, rotten sacking or well-dried touchwood can all be used for fuel.

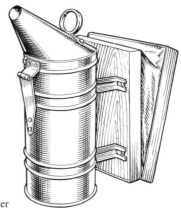

Bent-nose smoker

Veil It is very painful to be stung round the eyes, nose and mouth, and if one is assured that this cannot happen, more confidence is felt when hives are being examined.

Veils are made of black net or wire cloth, and should be worn with a bee suit; a boiler suit or 'bib and brace' makes a very suitable dress for either sex, as it can be washed to remove stains of honey, propolis or wax and can be fitted with a zip or Velcro fastening.

Gloves Those who are very sensitive to stings can wear gloves, but they must be supple leather gauntleted ones.

14

Veil with wire front

Hive tool and scraper

Hive tool and scraper   A hive tool for prising off covers and supers and loosening frames is another essential. It is made of steel and, besides its use as a lever, it forms a screwdriver at one end and at the other is widened and curved into a scraper. Failing this, a stout firmer chisel or screwdriver will serve most purposes. A scraper such as used by paper-hangers is also valuable for cleaning up covers and hive interiors, as well as being useful in handling honeycomb.

Manipulating cloths   It is very helpful to have two or three clean hessian bags at hand when manipulating stocks. One of these can be thrown over an open hive at a moment's notice without injuring bees. If this is done when signs of truculence are noticed, the outbreak is smothered at the start, and in a few moments' time more smoke can be given and the work continued. If a stock is divided into two for any reason, the part not being examined can be covered in the same way, so that it is not at the mercy of robbers. Something may have to be fetched from store, or a slight repair may be necessary. If a supered stock is being examined, the removed supers should be covered in this way and the risk of interference from outside will be greatly reduced.

These precautions and quiet, unhurried, methodical working, will make all the difference between a peaceful apiary and one which is a menace to the neighbourhood.

Tool box

It is essential that everything needed should be on hand when one opens a hive and to make sure of this, it is best to have a box made of plywood. Measuring 15 in (38 cm) each way, a size that will enable you to catch a swarm in it or hang combs taken out of a hive temporarily, it will hold all the things you need when at work: smoker, hive tool, bottle of syrup, dredger of flour (used for uniting colonies), knife, spare frame of foundation or comb, spare smoker fuel, and anything else which special work may require.

Record keeping

Every bee-keeper worth his salt keeps records, and if records are desirable, they should be well-kept. If the apiary contains only one stock, 'the bees' is sufficient description for it, but when the number increases, it is necessary to adopt some means of distinguishing one from another, and the simplest method is to number the stocks.

First, it should be clear that the number refers to the colony in a hive and not the hive itself. Numbers should, therefore, be movable. Appliance makers and ironmongers supply them in various styles, but a piece of zinc about 2 in (5 cm) square with the number painted

Portable tool box. *From left to right, rear row*: grass-cutting hook, smoker. *Centre*: smoker fuel, uncapping fork, secateurs, screwdriver, goose-wing bee brush. *Front row*: cover cloths, mouse guard, queen cages, hammer and hive tools

16

in white will do. One tack driven through a hole in the top will serve to affix it and it can be easily removed.

If we have numbered our stocks and our records to match, we had better keep the records indoors. We can then go through them at any time and see exactly what needs attention. On a clipboard keep the record sheets in numerical order. Before visiting the hives, go through the sheets, take out those which indicate that the colony needs attention and put them on top, returning them to proper order when the work is done. A pencil tied to the clip is always handy.

Weighing system For the bee-keeper who aims to get more exact information about the colony's performance, a system of weighing the hives is most illuminating. Not until one has practised weighing for a season, does one realize the peculiar manner in which the nectar-flow fluctuates and discover that what seem to us favourable conditions are often quite the reverse. Weighing is almost the only way of testing the reaction of bees to certain circumstances, or the influence of various factors, like situation, variety of bee, type of hive and so on. There is also a practical side. Weighing enables us to time the application of supers or to feed at critical moments.

Platform scales are expensive and not too portable, though they are the best for the purpose, because the hive does not need to be disturbed, but only one hive can be weighed at a time.

Graph of weighing records which shows the normal nectar-flow and the June gap

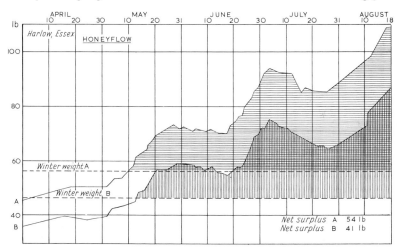

For many years Mr Mace used a spring balance which accommodated 120 lb (54·5 kg) and showed half-pound (0·23 kg) variations. The hives were in a shed, and the balance fixed to an iron rod 6 ft (2 m) above the ground, so that it could be moved along to weigh any one of five hives. The floor of each hive had four strong eyelets, one at each corner screwed into the side. Through these a rope sling was threaded and this hung on the hook of the balance. To facilitate lifting, the balance was attached to a pair of pulleys and a sash line ran through these for hauling. It took very few minutes to weigh the whole five and record the weights on a card.

A suitable workshop

In order to remove honey successfully it is important to obtain the necessary equipment, which must be all in readiness before the work begins. Bee-keepers with only one or two hives may be able to manage without a specially fitted room or hut for the indoor part of the work, but they should remember that honey is a food, so that scrupulous cleanliness must be observed in the extraction and bottling processes. Running water should be available for washing the hands and the tools used. Another factor to be considered is that bees—and wasps—have an unerring nose for honey and will soon invade any enclosure not specially designed to keep them out. On these grounds, as well as that of efficiency, it is desirable to have a place solely devoted to apiary work and preferably outside the dwelling house.

Equipment for extracting

Two important items of furniture are required, besides the actual machinery for extracting. The first is a work table, which should be firm and solid.

The other item is a small bee-proof cupboard in which supers of honey can be deposited, so that if the outer door is left open, they will be quite safe.

The fewer gadgets you are encumbered with during extracting the better, but the following are essential tools.

Honey extractor The honey extractor is a cylindrical tank of stainless steel or plastic, provided with a set of cages attached to a spindle, which revolves in the middle of the tank, the power being

18

transmitted by chain or cog gearing. Small sizes are operated by hand, but larger ones are fitted with electric motors. There are now three different types, the oldest and still the most widely used being the 'tangential' type, in which the cages are parallel with the sides of the tank. These are made to take from two shallow frames to four standard or eight shallow frames.

Another form is the 'radial extractor', in which the cages are so arranged that the frames radiate outwards from the spindle. When using the tangential, only one side of the comb can be extracted at once and it is necessary to lift all combs out and turn them round to do the other side. The radial extracts both sides at once.

The third type is the 'parallel radial' machine in which the spindle is horizontal instead of vertical and the combs turn over and over instead of round and round.

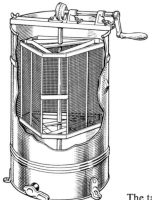

The tangential extractor

The basic principle of the extractor is that rapid revolution of the combs causes the honey to fly outwards against the tank wall and run down to the bottom, where it can be drawn off through a tap.

If the extractor is a small one, it can stand on the floor, but in this position the tap is too low down to allow a receptacle for honey to be put under it and it must afterwards be lifted onto a stand for this purpose. For a larger machine it is essential to have a stand raised at least 12 in (30 cm) from the ground. It must be heavy, as the machine is liable to rock at high speed. Where the floor is of cement, another plan is to dig out a pit to hold a honey tin or pail. One

19

Left: honey settling tank

Below: Pratley uncapping tray

advantage of the parallel radial is that its outlet is well above the ground.

Settling tank   Formerly called a 'ripener', the settling tank is a tall metal vessel, holding from 56 lb (25 kg) upwards, into which the honey from the extractor is transferred. It has a large container at the top with a perforated bottom to strain the honey and retain the coarser particles of wax. This is also fitted with a tap at the bottom. The advantage of this vessel is that straining goes on without attention. Alternatively you can use a supply of large honey tins, holding 14 lb (6·3 kg) or 28 lb (12·7 kg), but you will then have to strain the honey in the open by hanging a cone-shaped strainer on the extractor tap.

Uncapping   Before combs can be emptied of honey, the cappings must be removed. For this purpose a long sharp knife is required. A good carver is little inferior to the special knives sold and a saw-bladed bread knife is also an excellent tool. Two such knives should be used and they must be kept hot by standing them in a vessel of hot water. Knives heated by steam or electricity are also obtainable.

Uncapping has to be done over a vessel to catch the honey and wax removed. A rather elaborate, but useful, uncapping vessel is the Pratley tray, which is fitted with a water jacket, kept hot by an electric

20

element. This melts both honey and wax as they come from the knife and they run off into a vessel placed below, the wax rising and forming a cake on top of the honey.

If expense is an obstacle, you can manage very well with one or two large meat tins, fitted with draining grids. As these are filled, the contents are turned into the settling tank top. A paper-hanger's scraper is the best tool to scrape honey from tins, or for lifting masses of sticky cappings.

The Porter escape

One of the most useful inventions connected with bee-keeping is the Porter escape. This is a metal tunnel fitted with a pair of light springs, which meet at one end and afford passage one way only. The bees enter the open end of the tunnel, press the springs apart as they pass through, and the springs close behind them. This appliance is fitted into a board large enough to cover the brood-chamber. It is an advantage to have two or more such escapes in the board, so that

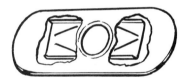

Porter escape

Super-clearer fitted with Porter escape

more bees can pass at the same time. The apparatus is used solely to clear honey supers of bees before removal, and is therefore known also as a 'super-clearer' (for instructions on its use, see page 47).

3 Selecting an Apiary Site

Hive sites

Before setting up a hive, choose a suitable place for it. It is important to select the place carefully at first, as bees cannot readily be moved during the active season. Two things have to be considered: the comfort of the bees and the convenience, not to say safety, of neighbours and members of your own family.

Bees always fly direct to a point they wish to reach, so that if there is a field of clover two hundred yards (180 m) from the hive and nothing in the line of flight, they will keep low down. If there is a wall or fence between, they will rise just high enough to clear the obstacle and no more.

When there is any doubt, or experience shows that passers are continually going through the bees' line, the problem can be solved by the erection of screens enclosing the hives in as much space as possible. A height of 6–8 ft (2–2·5 m) is sufficient.

In a garden you must also consider how far the necessary cultural work will be affected. To stand the bees in front of a plot where weeding and so on must be done constantly will be sure to cause annoyance, so the ground in front should be planted with something like potatoes or fruit bushes, which will need only occasional

The bees' line of flight can be directed for convenience and safety

attention, and this may be given in the evening or early morning when there is not much traffic from the hives.

A sheltered south slope Hives should always be placed so that they are sheltered from strong winds. As these usually come from north-west to south-west in summer, the best site is a south slope. Avoid any gap between buildings, where there is likely to be a strong draught. If there is a copse or similar shelter on the north or west side, so much the better. The object is to ensure that the air immediately about the hives is calm. The entrance of the hive should face south or south-east, though this is not a very important point, and where many hives are kept it is sometimes desirable to have them facing different directions.

Hives may be placed close together, but they should be far enough apart—say 3 or 4 ft (1–1·2 m)—to enable one to be attended to without interfering with the others. Where space permits, more room should be allowed. It is notable that when placed in a row, hives at the leeward end are stronger than those to windward, owing to drifting of bees along the line.

Out-apiaries

Most bee-keepers have to distribute their stocks, so as to have, at the outside, not more than 30 in one place. They will scarcely be able to make a living from less than 300 stocks, so they must have what are called 'out-apiaries'. Even the enthusiastic amateur may also

An out-apiary sheltered in a disused chalk pit

find it desirable, if he lives in a town, to keep most of his bees in a more rewarding area.

Suitable sites   It is not always easy to find sites for out-apiaries. Still, given a friendly approach, it will generally be found possible to rent a site which is not suitable for normal cultivation. Rough corners which it does not pay to plough, old gravel pits or quarries, a clearing in a wood or beside a copse or orchard, are often ideal places for bees. The fruit grower who recognizes the importance of bees in pollination and the growers of seed crops will be very willing to accommodate a few stocks.

The site should be accessible. If hives and supers of honey have to be transported over rough ground, or worse still, manhandled a considerable distance, it is easy to imagine the labour entailed. On the other hand, if the place is too easily reached, you never know who may come along and 'lift' the crop. Whatever the nature of the site, it must be protected against farm stock. Horses or cattle can soon upset hives. The cost of a few stout stakes and wire fencing will be a fairly cheap insurance against such disasters.

Moving the apiaries

Apart from keeping bees in out-apiaries, there is the possibility of moving them to certain crops at favourable times. It may well be profitable to take the stocks to a field of clover, field beans or oil seed rape in August, and leave them there until the blossom is over. It is more usual to take them to the larger fruit orchards in spring and to the moors in autumn. There is considerable difference between the two, for while the purpose of migration to fruit blossom is to fertilize the flowers, bees are taken to the heather in the hope of a crop of this most remunerative honey. The prospect of sufficient crop to repay the cost of moving to fruit blossom is rather remote and it is recognized that the bee-keeper requires a fee for bees placed in orchards.

Moving bees, as may be expected, is not a task to be undertaken lightly and, unless due regard is paid to certain rules, is liable to occasion trouble. Bees locate their home so exactly that they cannot find it if it is moved more than a few feet, and movement in the home apiary should be made by steps of not more than a yard (1 m) a day. As such moves have often to be made, it is most useful to have some convenient means of doing it. Hives are heavy for most of the year and merely to lift one with supers on is as much as most people can manage single-handed; to carry one any distance is out of the question. However, a hive can be carried by two people any reasonable distance, if two ropes are passed round it, one near each end and a couple of poles passed between cords and roof. The bearers can then lift the poles on to their shoulders.

In emergency, a stock can be moved to any new position at one go by shutting the hive up for three days. In the evening perforated zinc is put over the entrance and a board propped in front to shade it from sun. In hot weather ventilation must also be given by some other means, the best being to replace the usual cover by one of wire cloth. After three days' confinement bees seem to lose their memory and they locate the new position, as a swarm will always do if put down on a new site in the same apiary. This is the best method to follow if the stock is to be moved anywhere within a mile. If the distance is more than a mile and less than two, it will suffice to stuff grass into the entrance before the move. The bees have to dig their way out and this seems to make them aware they are in a new spot, which they memorize before starting work again. Outside the two-mile radius no precautions are necessary to ensure orientation of the new home. Bees should never be closed in till all have ceased flying for the day.

Transporting the hives It is in the matter of moving bees that single-walled hives score most heavily over the double-walled types, for the latter make greater demands on space in a vehicle. Single-walled hives of the National type present no difficulty. Appliance makers supply clamps which fix the parts securely together, entrance closers of perforated zinc and a special ventilating cover. To provide ample ventilation is most important and the only satisfactory way is to replace the wooden inner cover by one of wire gauze or perforated zinc. Bottom ventilation, however large, is not sufficient, for bees will crowd round it in their desire to escape and thus block it up. Full ventilation on top is the only safe plan.

In cool weather the roofs can be put over the ventilating screen, providing it is raised by sticks or blocks to allow air to circulate freely. In hot weather it is better to leave them off and provide some light covering to prevent the light from exciting the bees.

4 Nectar Sources

Even in his first season, the observant bee-keeper will not fail to notice great variation in the bees' activity. One day they will pour from the hive incessantly. The next perhaps only an odd bee or so is seen outside. Even on any one day there may be little activity, except for a single hour, when it seems as though foragers could not get out fast enough; sometimes one stock will be working hard, while others are quite sluggish.

Weather, flowers and nectar

The response to warmth and moisture is not alike in all plants. Just as some seeds germinate at temperatures as low as 40 °F (4 °C), while others require 90 °F (32 °C), so some flowers yield nectar freely when the mean temperature is no more than 45 °F (7 °C), while others require a day temperature of 70 °F (21 °C) before they begin to secrete. Generally speaking, these nectar-yielding minima correspond with the time of year at which the various plants blossom. The fruit trees, which bloom in spring, yield nectar at much lower temperatures than summer-blooming plants like clover.

The annual succession begins with the willows, the first being the sallow or goat willow. The white and crack willows follow and are less noticed, because of their height, but bees are active among them and often bring in quantities of honey.

Nectar crops

Fruit blossom begins at much the same time, the earliest being almond and peach. Plums do not seem quite so attractive, but cherry, pear and apple trees are great favourites and in good weather a strong stock of bees will gather considerable quantities from them. Apples give amber honey of quality and since cross-pollination is essential for a good crop of fruit the benefit of keeping bees in orchards is twofold.

Currants and gooseberries are also well worked. Hawthorn is a

26

common and long-blooming tree, rather uncertain in nectar yield, while the insignificant blossom of holly yields freely and constantly. Maple and sycamore are the last of the early-blooming trees to provide nectar in quantity.

Above: Caucasian bee collecting nectar from holly (*Ilex* sp.)
Above right: Italian bee collecting pollen from red-clover blossom

In April dandelions gild the meadows and one can see by the big loads of pollen brought in, how valuable this handsome weed is to bees. It is probably the major source of pollen at the time brood rearing is at its height, but it also yields abundant nectar.

During April and May cabbages bloom in gardens and allotments to give a nectar that crystallizes very quickly and coarsely so that it often cannot be extracted from the comb.

In early June there is a gap in the succession of nectar crops, so that colonies are often hard pressed to get enough for their needs and fall back on reserves.

The next plant of importance is the raspberry, which has a long blooming period, but is at its best about the beginning of June. Where this fruit is grown in quantity, it is most useful for tiding over the June gap. Field beans yield nectar plentifully and consistently and will often add substantially to the surplus.

Outshining all the clovers is the white, creeping, or Dutch clover which grows not only where sown in permanent or temporary pastures, but by roadsides and waste places everywhere in its wild form. It is particularly abundant on chalk hills like the Chilterns and the South Downs, and it is in such districts that the largest and purest crops of white clover honey are gathered. This honey is highly esteemed for its delicate flavour and attractive amber colour.

Lucerne is another leguminous plant which is a good nectar yielder on suitable limestone soils, but it does not figure very largely in our bee-keepers' estimation, mainly because in Britain it is rarely allowed to flower.

During the first half of July the main nectar-flow reaches its peak with the blossoming of the lime trees, whose scent often pervades the air during hot summer days. In favourable weather, large quantities of honey are gathered from these trees and they are particularly valuable in and around towns.

In August there may be a fair amount of surplus from red clover or sainfoin. Brambles also yield fairly consistently and in some places the woodland willow herb or fireweed adds its pale honey to the quota.

Honeydew

After these crops, there are in most districts few plants which can be relied on to add much to the surplus, but at this time, especially in very hot weather, bees sometimes collect large quantities of 'honey-dew'. This is not true nectar, but a sugary exudation from the leaves of many plants, notably lime trees and oaks, said to be induced by the attacks of aphis and other piercing insects. Honeydew varies a good deal in colour and flavour, but is always darker than floral honey. Moreover, it often contains sooty particles, which may either be actual soot deposited on the leaves, or the product of a fungus. The bees appear to like this substance and, indeed, its flavour is often quite agreeable, but it is considered to be liable to cause dysentery in bees in winter.

Not much can be done about honeydew, but when extracting, the presence of this in the combs can usually be detected by holding them up to the light; such combs should either be kept in store for feeding back to bees in spring—not in autumn—or extracted and kept separately for use in cooking.

Heather honey

Only one other substantial source of honey is likely to be met with in these islands and that is confined to peaty and sandy soils; in such places the characteristic plant is heather which, under favourable conditions, gives immense quantities of honey. There are several

28

species, the ling, bell heather and crossleaved heath. The last two produce dark honey, not otherwise different from what the Scots call 'flower-honey', but ling produces a peculiar jelly-like honey which rarely if ever crystallizes. Heather blooms from mid-July to late September. In Scotland it is looked upon as the main crop and special steps are taken to secure the largest possible harvest from it.

The production of heather honey requires a technique which differs considerably from that used in getting the crop from clover, and those who live in districts where the latter is of small account must manage their bees very differently. It is quite useless to build up a big population for the clover and hope that the same bees will gather as much from the heather, for not only will the clover foragers be worn out, but the peak of brood-rearing will have so long passed that there will be comparatively few young bees reaching the foraging stage.

There are, of course, some areas like Dartmoor, the Surrey Hills, parts of the New Forest and a few other districts where heather grows in sufficient profusion, but here it can best be looked upon as a supplementary crop, valuable for providing winter stores, instead of being the main object as it is in real moorland counties.

Another handicap is that days are shorter and nights longer than during the clover flow. Sometimes, of course, August is a very hot month, but equally often it is wet and sometimes cold. For this reason it is seldom wise to rely on bees building comb at the heather. It is far better to mobilize all built-out comb, and take this along with the bees. It will always result in a larger surplus of heather honey.

Those who live in or near the moors will be in the best position to obtain sites: taking bees to the heather and bringing them home again will be part of their normal procedure. For those strange to the moorland country, living at a distance, the whole thing will be a gamble, for they will have to find suitable standing ground, either by a preliminary visit or by correspondence. Members of bee-keepers' associations will find it best to get in touch with the association secretary in the moorland district chosen. The cost of moving the bees out and home again will also have to be considered.

Again, those who live at a distance will most likely not be able to visit the hives often, if at all, unless they find quarters in the neighbourhood and make a heather holiday of the enterprise. In these circumstances, all the supers the stocks are likely to need should be put on at the start. Excluders are not necessary, as there is very little danger of the queen needing more breeding space than she has in the brood-chamber. Two shallow frame supers or section racks will normally be ample and they can be put on before the move. In hot weather this will be an advantage, since it provides more ventilation. Needless to say there should be a fairly good supply of honey in the brood-chamber in case conditions should be bad, but combs overloaded with new honey would be dangerous on the journey in hot weather.

Once in a while bees swarm at the heather but it is sufficiently unusual to be negligible. If a good crop has been secured and the brood-chamber as well as supers filled up, the trouble of feeding will have been saved, but it is well to remember that there are some years when they are likely to return lighter than when they set out, in which case feeding will be necessary. It is therefore best not to delay too long in bringing them home.

Planting for bees

New bee-keepers often ask what they should plant for their bees and although it is not profitable to grow plants *only* for this purpose, there is no reason why garden flowers should not include some of those most favoured by bees. No music is more delightful to the bee-lover than the hum of foragers in a cotoneaster bush, or a bed of mignonette.

Suitable plants SHRUBS Berberis, buckthorn, buddleia, cotoneaster, erica, genista, ribes, snowy mespilus, snowberry, veronica
PERENNIALS AND BIENNIALS Anchusa, arabis, aubrieta, campanulas, Canterbury bells, crane's-bill, centaurea, forget-me-not, French honeysuckle, globe thistle, hollyhock, linaria, mallow, Michaelmas daisy, nepeta, rose-bay, salvias, sidalcea, sedums, veronica, verbascum, violet, wallflower
SUMMER BEDDING PLANTS Dahlias, fuchsia, heliotrope
BULBS Crocus, hyacinth, narcissus, snowdrop
ANNUALS Borage, cornflower, clarkia, gilia, limnanthes, mignonette, phacelia, poppy, scabious

5 Establishing a Colony

Nucleus colonies are sent out in travelling boxes, in which the combs are kept in place by a lid of perforated zinc in a frame, screwed down to the sides of the box. On arrival it should be carried to the place where the hive awaits it. If the weather is bad, or it is not convenient

Travelling box

to transfer the bees to the hive, stand the box close to the hive, and open the entrance hole in front, so that the bees are free to come and go. Something should be put over the box to keep out rain, and it can be left till a suitable day for the transference.

Transferring from the travelling box

The middle of a nice warm day is most suitable. First light the smoker and see that it is working properly. On no account put off doing this until the veil has been donned; at least one fatal accident has been caused by setting fire to the veil while lighting the smoker. If you do not wear gauntlet gloves, fasten the coat cuffs closely, so that bees cannot crawl up the sleeves, and secure the bottoms of your trousers. It is as well to get into the habit of protecting yourself properly, as there are times when bees fall to the ground and climb up the handiest object.

Now take out the screws which fasten the cover of the box, puff a smoke through the perforations and, after three minutes, take off the lid gently.

The combs may then be lifted out, starting with an outside one, which should be put in the hive in the same position as it occupied in the box, the others being taken in turn and put close up against each other. Each comb is lifted by gripping the projecting ends firmly and

Transferring live bees from a travelling box into a National hive. A cover cloth has been laid over the combs already transferred

raising it steadily and gently till it is clear of the box. If lifted till level with the face, one side can be examined. To see the other side, turn it in the direction shown in the diagram opposite; it is wise to keep it always vertical. This method of turning combs is quite simple and becomes a habit in time.

This is the best
method of turning
combs

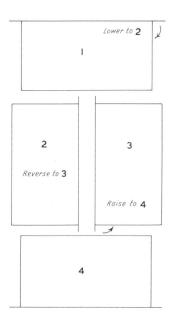

Examining the comb Take a good look at each comb as it is removed. The outer ones will have sealed and unsealed stores, but the
inner ones should have brood in the centre. Some will be capped
over and should present a dull even surface of yellow or pale-brown
colour. Unsealed cells will have white plump curled-up grubs, some
filling the cell, others lying in the bottom. There should also be little
white eggs in many cells. The middle combs should have honey
along their tops and extending down the sides. It is as well to see
the queen, so that one may be sure she has been put in the hive, but
there is no need to be unduly anxious about her. Beginners often fail
to find her, especially if she is young and active, but if there are eggs
she is pretty sure to be there. After all the combs have been transferred
any bees remaining in the box should be shaken into the hive by
turning the box upside down over it and thumping it vigorously.
The cover board is then put over the frames, the roof over this, and
all should be well.

If there is plenty of honey in the combs and the weather is fine,
nothing further is required, but if there seems to be very little food
and the weather is not favourable, a feeder should be put on and a
good supply of syrup given. Syrup is made by putting 2 lb (1 kg) of

33

white sugar into 1 pint (568 ml) of boiling water and stirring till melted. Various methods of feeding will be described later on, but a good makeshift feeder is a honey jar. After filling this with syrup, put two thicknesses of muslin over and tie down, or fasten with a stout rubber band. Turn the jar upside down and over the feedhole and leave till emptied, which will be in a day or so, according to the strength of the colony.

Hiving a swarm

Swarms are sent out in boxes or skeps and have to be hived in a different manner from stocks or nuclei. First it will be necessary to have prepared frames of foundation. These may be bought all ready for use, or made up. For a swarm of not less than 4 lb (1·8 kg), the full complement of ten frames should be used and the brood-chamber filled up with them. A smaller swarm should have less, say six, others being added later as it completes them.

Having filled the brood-chamber and put the cover on it, lift it from the floor and stand it on one side. In its place put an empty brood-chamber, or shallow super. Take the cover off the box or skep containing the swarm. Hold it mouth down over the empty chamber,

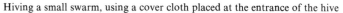

Hiving a small swarm, using a cover cloth placed at the entrance of the hive

and jerk the bees into it. Put the prepared brood-chamber over it and leave until the bees have climbed up and settled among the frames. They will do this by evening and the empty chamber can be removed, one person holding the full one up while another takes the empty one away. This plan is better than the one of throwing the swarm in front of the hive, for it can be done at any time without fear of the bees taking wing.

Unless there is a heavy nectar-flow on, it is wise to feed swarms generously for the first few days.

Opening the hive

Before opening a hive, have everything ready for the operation to be performed and be quite sure you know what you are going to do. Hives should not be opened without a definite purpose and that should be carried out without interruption. If it is absolutely necessary to leave in the middle of a job, the cover should be put over the combs and the roof replaced. On no account should brood combs be left exposed, either to cold or the sun, more than can be avoided.

Bees behave quite differently at different times. When the weather is warm and nectar is abundant they are quite amiable and need scarcely any subjugation. On cold windy days when foraging is at a standstill they behave very differently, often rushing out to sting the moment the cover is lifted. Thundery weather is also notoriously irritating to them. Such times should not be chosen for opening hives if it can be avoided. In the autumn great care should be taken, not only to subdue the colony before operating, but to prevent robber bees from other hives attacking it.

Stings and their treatment   The bee-keeper, while doing all he can to avoid stings, must bear them bravely if they are received during an operation, carry on and finish the job, or at least replace everything taken from the hive and cover up properly before leaving. The effect of stings depends a good deal on the individual constitution, but as a rule, swelling increases for twenty-four hours and subsides during the next twenty-four. Local swelling need cause no alarm, though it may be very great. The effect of a sting may be made worse by treatment. Most people try and pull it out, but this presses the poison bag and squeezes more into the wound. The proper way is to *scrape* the sting off with the thumbnail or a knife.

Various things are advocated as treatment. Iodine, ammonia, onion juice, tobacco, and several proprietary remedies, rarely do more than allay irritation, and a little honey smeared on is just as effective. In the case of great swelling, hot fomentation is the most effective treatment. Serious results are not unknown and a few people are so allergic to stings that they are liable to collapse. Medical aid must be sought in such cases. After a few stings have been received, nine people out of ten become more or less immune and all but indifferent to them.

Supering

The beginner should not be too disappointed if he fails to secure honey for himself in the first season, though if he starts with a full stock in April, he should certainly get some in an average year. If he gets a working knowledge of the first principles of the craft and builds up a good stock for the future, the novice may well be content.

A June nucleus on four combs will rarely do more than build up its strength during the main nectar-flow, and it will not be necessary to do more than add frames of foundation one by one until the brood-box is full.

Full stocks and swarms will require 'supering', that is to say, when the brood-chamber is all but full of bees and brood, another chamber is added above it. It will have been noticed at the very first inspection of the combs that bees put their honey at the top as far as possible from the entrance, or on the combs outside the area in which the queen breeds. It does not always remain where it was first placed. Foragers put it in the empty cells which come handiest, as they are eager to go and get more. It is very thin stuff and it is partly by being moved about that it loses its water content and becomes thick and viscid. The house bees carry away any in the centre combs so that the queen may use the cells for breeding and they naturally take it higher up as the brood spreads out. By putting surplus chambers on top we conform to the bees' habits, at the same time ensuring that surplus will be in the most convenient place for removal.

Supers and seasons How often supers are needed depends on the season, which is unpredictable, but it should be a rule never to let bees run short of room. It can do no harm to put a super on before it is actually needed, but to delay doing so when the brood-nest is full will almost certainly cause a swarm. In the height of a good season a stock will gather from 4–10 lb (1·8–4·5 kg) of nectar daily. As a standard comb only holds about 5 lb (2 kg) of matured honey, it is obvious that the space available in the brood-chamber for the thin and light nectar coming in will soon be choked. It is a fairly sound rule to put on a super as soon as the first bees begin to appear on the two outer combs of the brood-box.

Adding a super   Adding a super is a simple matter. First remove the hive roof. If it is a flat one, turn it upside down beside the hive and stand the super on the edges of this improvised tray by turning it at a slight angle. Insert the hive tool under a corner of the wooden

Adding a wooden-framed queen excluder

Adding a second super. The bees have been smoked off the first super

cover and lever it up gently, puffing in a little smoke to drive the bees down. Lift the cover and put it on top of the super. There will be bees adhering to it, but they will not be crushed if the cover is lowered gently. Now send a waft of smoke across the open brood-chamber and as soon as the bees have run down, lift the super and place it in position. To avoid crushing bees, first put one edge on the corresponding part of the brood-box and then lower gently. Sometimes the bees build pieces of comb on top of the frames: these should be scraped off with the hive tool and dropped into the tool box. If excluder is to be used, it must be laid correctly over the brood-chamber before the super. If it is lifted up and down two or three times, bees on top of the frames will soon get out of the way.

Sections

Sections are small wooden frames in which comb for eating is built, and are made of fine white bass-wood, imported from the U.S.A. They reach the bee-keeper as flat strips grooved across in three places and dovetailed at the ends. There are two styles—four bee-way and two bee-way.

Each section is filled with a full sheet of specially thin foundation, which can be had either cut to exact size, or in strips from which three can be cut. Small strips of the same material can be used as 'starters', which greatly reduces the outlay.

To fold sections a frame or 'block' which exactly holds one is used, so as to ensure a perfect square. But first, to avoid breakage in folding, the cross grooves must be moistened. Stand the section in the block, grooves inwards, so that the split top projects and fix the half with the bevel on top sloping away from you. Fix the square of foundation on this bevel so that it is quite level and barely touches the bottom, sliding it down the grooves—if any. Press the top firmly against the bevel. This is important, for if it is not so secured, the sheet will probably buckle when the other half of the top is pressed down into its dovetails.

As completed, the sections are put in the racks and thin metal or wood partitions are placed between each row. The last row has a board pressed close against it by a spring. Too much care cannot be used to get sections square, with flat foundation and the dividers properly adjusted.

It is useless to put a section rack on early in the season. The best super to give first is always either a standard or shallow frame super and not until the main flow arrives and the bees are working eagerly in this, should a section rack be added. Bees can often be tempted into the section rack by putting one or two partly filled sections in the centre; unfinished sections from one season can thus be used for the next. If it fills rapidly, another can be added when it is half full. An empty section rack should never be put under a half-filled one, but when the bees have well started in the second it is a very good idea to transpose them, for the first will then have less traffic over it and can be removed immediately it is seen to be well sealed.

In a really good season, this plan should result in a satisfactory crop, but in moderate seasons it will rarely procure anything like full racks. In such conditions, use a stock which has nearly filled two brood-chambers. When the main flow begins take off the top chamber and remove from both all combs except those containing brood and only enough of them to fill one chamber. Give the rest to weaker stocks in the apiary. All bees are shaken back into the brood-chamber.

Having put an excluder over the brood-chamber, put on two racks of sections at once. Both will be filled with bees immediately and, given fair weather, they draw out rapidly.

Even so, you must be on guard. If a change for the worse in the weather takes place, the stock will be practically foodless, so it is a wise precaution to tuck away any honeycombs taken out at the start of the operation, and put them back on top at the first sign of bad weather.

If you do not care to risk trying for sections only, it is always possible to get a few in a shallow super by using a hanging frame into which three sections can be fitted. It is not difficult to fit three sections into an ordinary shallow frame, wedging up any gaps securely so that there is no room for the bees to build burr comb.

Cut comb

A great many of the disadvantages of sections can be avoided, however, by the production of 'cut comb'. The method is to insert frames fitted with thin unwired foundation into supers between good, straight, fully drawn combs, preferably just before an expected nectar-flow. The bees will rapidly draw out, fill and cap the cells without displaying the reluctance so often found in the case of sections.

6 Swarms and Swarming

The experienced bee-keeper cannot always recognize the imminence of this event by outward signs, so it is no wonder that the novice is taken by surprise, or that sometimes a swarm disappears without his knowing it, so that the harvest of honey he saw being built up turns out to be little more than a mirage.

The earliest sign is the appearance of drones. After a while you may notice that the bees are not rushing out of the hive as eagerly as before and there is a tendency to cluster about the entrance. Although this does not necessarily mean imminent swarming, it shows that nectar sources are not at the moment abundant, and if it is intended to adopt any of the measures described further on, this is the time to examine the stocks to see if queen cells have been started. At the same time it is well to repeat that stocks sometimes swarm without showing any sign of slacking off.

January to May

From January to May there is a gradual increase of flowers and the growth of bee colonies coincides with this. Towards the end of May spring blossom passes its peak and there is a decline in nectar income, so that there is generally a short period when bees consume as much as they gather daily. It is during this period that prime swarms usually appear and it is not a coincidence, for the slackening of bloom checks the foraging instinct and causes the hive to become more congested.

May to June

Real prime swarms generally appear from mid-May to mid-June, according to the state of the season.

If nothing is done to a stock which has thrown a prime swarm, it will often send out a second swarm or 'cast' when the young queens are ready to fly. This is usually about nine days after the prime swarm issued, but it may happen before if the swarm was delayed. In bad weather the bees keep mature young queens in their cells till a fine day comes, and it is then not unusual for one or more to leave with the swarm.

Collecting a swarm

Once the swarm has settled, it should be collected at once. The traditional receptacle is a straw skep, which is roomy and light, no

A swarm that has drawn comb. Skep hives were widely used before frame hives

This inverted skep shows how bees build and attach their combs. The large cells at the lower edge on one comb are queen cells

small advantage if the swarm has to be taken from a place only reached from a ladder; but a clean odourless cardboard box may also be used.

A swarm on a bough near the ground is easily taken. Holding the box beneath it, the operator seizes the bough and shakes it vigorously, so that all the bees fall in. The box is then laid on the ground and turned over, a stick being put under one edge to allow bees to go in and out. If the queen is in, the others will soon follow: if not, they will come out and return to the bough. The operation must then be repeated. Sometimes shaking is impossible, as on a wall, post or tree trunk, from which it is necessary to brush them. A bunch of grass, or a stiff feather will serve.

The only suitable plan for removing a swarm from a hedge or thick bush is to prop the box over it and drive the bees up with smoke. It is even better to use a brood-chamber. Some frames of foundation or preferably combs, should be put in the chamber and covered with a sack. The brood-chamber is then placed as nearly as possible over the swarm and made secure by one or two props. When the bees have gone up, the brood-chamber can be placed directly in the position it is to occupy. Swarms on the ground are easily hived in the same way.

Swarms in trees give more trouble. Sometimes they are readily accessible from a ladder, but if they are on a slender bough this is not always feasible. It is sometimes possible to take them by fixing a skep or box on the tines of a pitchfork, raising this till the swarm is inside, and striking it sharply against the underside of the bough. Often the only way is to cut off the bough. Before doing so a rope should be fastened as near the swarm as possible, then passed over a bough above and brought to the ground, where one person holds it while another cuts the bough. It can then be gently lowered.

Value of swarms

Under the skep system of bee-keeping, prime swarms were looked upon as *the* producers of the harvest. The earlier they arrived the better. They were put into a completely empty hive, so the combs they built were quite new, or as they were called 'virgin'. Coming just before the main flow, swarms concentrate on foraging, raise little brood, and in a reasonably good summer, fill the hive with honey.

Under the modern system, bee-men are apt to make no distinction between swarms and stocks and often try to winter swarms with old queens, but it is a great mistake. Prime swarms should be made to concentrate on nectar gathering, and when the season for this has passed they should either be re-queened or broken up to strengthen nuclei of the current season.

Management of swarms

There are several ways of minimizing the ill effects of swarming. Early swarms, say those issuing before the second week of June, can be treated as separate stocks. If your apiary is full, it is not a bad plan to sell such swarms, which make a good price and leave you with a re-queened hive, which has every chance of regaining foraging strength before the main nectar-flow.

The oldest plan is to find the old queen in the swarm, kill her and return the swarm to the parent hive. Supers are added to allow ample storage space and if the nectar-flow is on, the stock will devote its energy to filling them. In due time a young queen will be mated to

Specially enlarged cells in which queens are raised

head the colony. This plan, however, has difficulties. There are usually several young queens in their cells and when the first is ready, she may leave the hive and take all the bees which swarmed before with her. To prevent this it is essential, before returning the swarm, to destroy all queen cells but one. If this is done properly it will prevent a second swarm, but as queen cells will be in all stages from sealed and ripe ones to others hardly started, it is easy to overlook some. To do the work properly, all the bees must be shaken from the combs. The cell retained should be the largest and most mature. A further risk is involved in this method. The virgin queen may be lost on her mating flight, or bad weather may delay her mating beyond the twenty days usually considered the limit of time during which she can be fertilized. She will then be a useless drone breeder and the stock will perish.

As a safeguard against this it is wise to save another queen cell in a nucleus colony. Two or three combs well covered with bees and one queen cell are put in an empty hive. The bees from one or two more combs are shaken in with them to make good the loss caused by older bees returning to the old home. If either queen fails to mate, the two lots can be reunited. If both survive, the nucleus can be built up to form a new colony.

The Pagden method   A system that enables the foraging bees to be kept in a single unit is what is known as the Pagden method, because it was originally described by J. W. Pagden in a booklet published in 1870. It is simplicity itself. Instead of putting the newly hived swarm on a fresh site, it is put on the stand occupied by the parent stock, which has been moved to a new site. The consequence is that the swarm is reinforced by all the bees flying at the time, for they naturally return to the known spot and for at least three days after hiving the swarm becomes stronger. Having been seriously depleted in numbers, the old stock rarely throws a second swarm.

This simple plan has been modified in many ways. Instead of moving the old stock right away, some put it beside the swarm, turning the entrance at right angles from the swarm. It is left thus for three days and then taken away to a fresh site. A further batch of foragers is added to the swarm in this way.

Swarm prevention

In some years swarming is very prevalent and nothing will stop it. Generally speaking, a fine dry summer has a short swarming period, while in a patchy season swarming is often protracted and tiresome. A good honey season is also a swarming season. To keep a strain of bees not inclined to excessive swarming, to have colonies headed always by young queens and to provide ample breeding room are the first steps to swarm prevention. They will not entirely stop it because, to have good crops of honey, we must induce bees to breed early and freely, so that when the nectar-flow comes there will be a greater proportion of adult bees, and this makes for the congestion which many regard as the main cause of swarming.

There are two main systems of swarm prevention: regular removal of queen cells, and artificial swarming or division of stocks.

Removal of queen cells   The late Dr C. C. Miller was the chief exponent of what he called the 'cell killing' method, now generally known as the 'ten-day' plan.

This method of going through all colonies every ten days to cut out all queen cells entails a lot of labour if stocks are, as they should be, full of bees and brood. If *any* cells are found, practically every comb must be searched to make sure all are destroyed, and since bees make a point of clustering thickly round queen cells, it is easy to overlook them unless the combs are shaken.

Artificial swarming   Artificial swarming is best done as an adjunct to the cell-killing plan, colonies being divided *only when queen cells are in an advanced stage*. It is the greatest possible mistake to interfere with colonies that show no sign of imminent swarming. They are almost certain to be the best nectar-gatherers and to divide their forces will cause disorganization and loss of crop. It is better to give such stocks more breeding space, either by the addition of a brood-chamber, or by removal of combs of sealed brood, giving these to weaker colonies and providing empty combs or frames of foundation. Even this should be done only to a very moderate extent, for every change disturbs the colony.

The bee-keeper who is a novice with only one hive may prefer to increase it to two or more rather than try for a good crop of honey during the first season. This justifies the division of a strong colony at the earliest moment, even when it shows no sign of swarming.

Clipping the queen's wings   Another method intended to prevent loss of swarms is clipping the queen's wings, so that if a swarm issues it remains close to the hive because the queen cannot fly. Those who practise clipping, operate while the queen is in the nucleus, as soon as the production of worker brood shows that she has been duly mated. Fine sharp scissors are used and the large wing on one side is cut about the middle. To do the work safely, the queen is picked up by the thorax—never by the abdomen. One blade of the scissors is slipped under the wings, care being taken not to include a leg. Another plan is to use a little wooden fork, across which a piece of thread is stretched. This is laid over the queen's thorax as she walks along the comb. Before clipping a queen for the first time, you should practise on a few drones. There is always some danger of bees super-seding a clipped queen—perhaps because of the mutilation.

7 The Honey Harvest

Removing the honey

More beginners get into trouble about removing the honey than from any other cause. They suppose that the bees will resent the operation and they are apt to put it off as long as possible. This is the very worst thing they can do. It may seem to the uninitiated that while bees are flying in large numbers they are most likely to be troublesome and that it is better to wait until they are quieter. In fact the reverse is true, for while there is active foraging, there are fewer bees at home during the day and these are comparatively young ones, much less likely to sting than the old hands. If all is quiet outside, the hive is packed full of bees and immediately the hive is opened, they rush out to repel marauders.

This chart of the honey season shows when the bees are most active. The weekly net gains of the two hives indicate that one is weak and the other strong

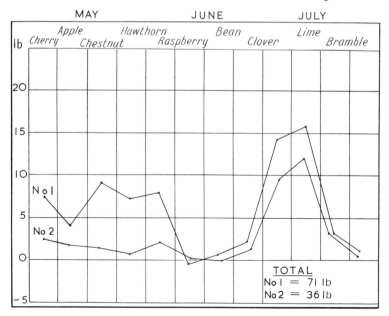

The secret of pacifying bees is to fill them up with honey by frightening them with smoke. They cannot fill up unless there is unsealed honey in the hive and every day after the nectar-flow is over, more and more honey is sealed and less and less is available. If the honey can be removed before the flow is quite over, it may be done fairly easily. The longer the work is postponed, the more the bees resent it.

When the time has come to remove the honey, it is best to choose a fine day when bees are busy, but it can be done at any time after the honey is sealed over. Unsealed honey is not properly ripe and if extracted at this stage will be thin and very liable to ferment in store. A few open cells in a well-capped comb do not matter, but the bulk of them should be fully sealed.

Opening up Having removed the roof of the hive and turned it upside down, as was done when adding supers, stand the super-clearer on it, making quite sure it is right way up so that bees can only pass down from above. Insert the hive tool under a corner of the super, lever it up and put in a piece of wood to support it while the other corner is lifted. It is best to choose the side that holds the frame ends. Puff in a little smoke and gently raise the super until you can see the frame ends. If any of these are sticking up, they must be pressed down and no attempt should be made to lift the super until all are quite free. Holding the super firmly—it may weigh 30 lb (13·7 kg), so it will not be a light task—give it a slight twist to free it finally from the brood-chamber and stand it on the clearer. Then lift board and super together and put them back on the hive. When you have made quite sure that there are no gaps round the super through which bees can pass, put the roof on and leave the hive alone for some hours. The time taken to clear a super varies, but if put on one day it will be clear the same time next day. It can then be removed—leaving the board in place for the time—and taken into the workshop or honey house.

If there are two or more supers on the hive they can all be cleared at once by putting the super-clearer under the lowest, but if they are both full, they will weigh little short of 60 lb (27 kg), so that it is a task for two persons or a very strong one.

This is the safest, most foolproof method of removing honey, but it has serious drawbacks. It is always desirable to get the honey extraction done in one operation and it is much easier if done in the middle of a warm day, for honey flows more readily then. If the clearer is put on in fine weather, it may be much cooler the next day when the super is removed. Moreover, if there are two or more supers on a hive and you cannot lift all at once, only one can be removed a day. If there are several hives, an escape board must be provided for each or the operation will be still more protracted.

Direct removal of combs for extraction Provide yourself with some empty super boxes and a few clean hessian bags, and make sure the smoker is well alight and with plenty of fuel to last an hour at least. The hive tool and a bee brush are the only other requirements. Beside the hive to be dealt with first, spread a bag on the ground and on this put an empty super box. Remove the roof and inner cover, which should be put upside down with the bees on it in front of the hive. Having puffed smoke into the super, loosen all the combs with the hive tool so that they come out easily. One by one take out the combs and shake them over the board in front of the hive. As each comb is cleared, put it in the empty super and when this is full, cover with another bag. Then remove the empty super from the hive. The second or it may be third super is dealt with in the same way. Finally, the inner cover is replaced on the brood-chamber. Each hive is treated thus, so that at the end there is a series of supers beside each hive, all safely covered with sacks.

There are a number of volatile chemicals which bees do not like and from which they retreat. Of these, benzaldehyde has been used with some success for clearing supers. The method of application consists in having some kind of absorbent pad mounted on the lower side of a clearer board onto which the chemical is sprinkled. The supers are then lightly smoked from above and the 'fume chamber' placed on top of the top super. The bees should move down about the depth of one super. The difficulty is that sometimes the bees do not go down if the weather is cold.

Removing sections The clearer board *must* be used for sections, not only because they cannot be shaken in the same way as combs, but also because you must not take the smallest risk of robbers, who would tear at the cappings and spoil their appearance. Sections also must be completely sealed, so they usually have to be left till the nectar-flow is over. In using the clearer it is most important to see that bees cannot get in or out other than through the escape.

Extracting honey

Having carried the honeycombs safely into the workshop, begin the
work of extracting at once. Be sure the machine is quite clean and
runs smoothly. It should be so placed that the uncapped combs can
be put into it without honey dripping on the floor. On a table, stand
the uncapping tray and just behind it the jug of hot water with the
two uncapping knives. It is a good idea to have a bucket of water
and some clean cloths in case your hands get too sticky.

Uncapping is not difficult when the knack has been acquired.
Holding the frame by one lug, rest the other on the support provided
in the tray, taking care that it does not slip. It should be tilted over
a little at the top on the side being cut. The hot knife is placed flat
on the frame below the comb and drawn downwards to slice the
capping off in one piece. The tilt will cause it to fall away from the

Uncapping with an electric knife

frame and drop into the tin. The comb is then turned round and the
other side cut in the same way. If parts of the comb do not project
beyond the wood they will have to be cut with the end of the knife,
after the main slice has fallen. Some bee-keepers prefer to use an
uncapping fork. This useful instrument has some twenty sharp tines
about 2 in (5 cm) long, often slightly cranked. The points of the tines
are inserted in the comb just below the cappings, which can then
be removed with great facility and a minimum of mess.

49

Still holding it by the lug, put the comb into the cage of the extractor. If this takes two shallows on a side, see that the first is well up to the end, or the second may not go in. Also make sure it is right down to the bottom, for in some machines a frame that sticks up slightly is likely to have its lug broken off when the cage is revolved; sometimes the metal ends get in the way and if they are at all loose it is better to remove them before uncapping. When the full number of combs the machine takes are in, the handle should be turned, gently at first and then faster till the honey can be heard pattering against the side of the machine. In a radial extractor, continue until it is judged that the combs are empty. In tangential machines, the combs must be turned round. If the combs are new, it is wise to run the machine gently and get part only of the honey from the first side, turning the comb to do the other and then turning again to finish the first side. To reverse the combs when each is in a separate cage, they must be lifted up, turned round and dropped in again. The emptied combs are put back in their boxes and other combs extracted until all have been done.

Meanwhile, the honey in the extractor must be drawn off as it accumulates and comes up to the level of the cages. It can be drawn into large tins and poured into the settling tank. If one has no tank, it must remain in the tins and should be strained later. Great caution is needed in straining, for honey runs slowly through the strainer and, if it is allowed to come out too fast, may run over the top or overfill the tin. It is a wise precaution to stand the tin in a good-sized meat dish. Honey runs quite silently and, if one is doing something else, it is easy to forget it. A proper settling tank is, for this reason alone, a worthwhile investment, as the extractor can be emptied quickly. After standing a few days in the settling tank, during which air bubbles, scraps of wax and so on will rise to the top, the honey is drawn off into tins.

Cleaning up is a job which should not be put off after the honey has been cleared from extractor and tins. If there is more than can be done in one day, there is no harm in leaving the things as they are for a day or so, but when all has been extracted the apparatus should be cleaned up at once.

To clean out the extractor, close the valve and pour in a gallon (4·5 litres) or so of tepid water. Swill this well round until all honey and wax has been washed off. Run the liquor into a tin and use it to rinse out the uncapping tin. This liquor can be saved to add to the washing of the cappings later on to make mead or honey vinegar.

Hot water can then be used to clean out the extractor, which should be dried thoroughly and stored with a cloth of some kind over it. It is an expensive piece of apparatus and will last a lifetime if proper care is taken of it, but it will soon be ruined if left with honey adhering to it.

One thing more remains to be done—the return of wet combs to the hives from which they came. This should not be done till evening, otherwise the smell of honey will attract robbers. The roof is removed and the hole in the cover is exposed sufficiently to let the bees come up. The super is put on, covered with a sack and the roof placed over it. In a few days the bees will clean and even repair the combs so that they can be stored away for use another year. They should be wrapped up in newspaper immediately, so that wax moth cannot reach them, for they are a most valuable asset.

The cappings in the settling tank will continue to part with honey for a few days if stirred up from time to time, but when honey no longer runs out the cappings should be turned into a large vessel with tepid water and allowed to stand for twenty-four hours. Stir occasionally to get as much honey out as possible. The liquor can be drained off and put with the other washing water to make mead. The wax is dried thoroughly and either melted down at once, or stored in a place safe from wax moth till it is convenient to deal with it.

Sections and cut comb

Sections and cut comb should be left till they are fully sealed before removal. In a really good season this does not take long, but in moderate or poor years they may have to wait a week or so after the flow is over and even then some will not be finished. They should not be left on after they are sealed, or they will be stained by the addition of propolis and added wax.

After removing sections by the aid of the clearer board, they must be taken from the rack carefully as they are easily damaged. The best plan is to use pieces of wood about 1 in (2·5 cm) square and long enough to go along a row of sections, inside the rack. After removing the spring and board which hold the sections tight, put the strips of wood under the rows, and press the edges of the rack down. This forces the sections up above the rack and they can be easily removed. Propolis and wax on the wood should be scraped off with a blunt knife and the sections packed temporarily in a tin.

When the combs for cut comb are sealed, they can be withdrawn and cut into pieces about $2\frac{5}{8}$ in $\times 3\frac{1}{2}$ in ($6\cdot6 \times 9$ cm). These will just fit into the plastic containers specially made for the purpose which are available from the appliance manufacturers. A well-filled piece of comb this size will weigh almost exactly 8 oz (220 g). Cutting tools specially made for the job can be had, but for bee-keepers producing only a small amount of cut comb, it is simple to do the cutting on a clean block of wood or similar surface. Use a cold, sharp kitchen knife and very little waste or mess will result. In the case of heather honey, owing to the thixotropic nature of the honey, no seepage at all will occur.

Extracting heather honey

Heather honey is quite different from any other. It is a thick jelly which cannot normally be extracted by machine. The recognized way of extracting heather honey is by a press. Several patterns are obtainable, but in each the comb, having been cut out of the frames and wrapped in muslin, is pressed until the honey is forced out and only a flat slab of wax remains.

Heather-honey press

There is a device which, by inserting a number of pins into the cells, temporarily breaks down the jelly so that it can be centrifugally extracted, but most people have found it a rather impracticable affair. It is far better to get the crop in sections, which are snowy white and always command top prices. Failing this, shallow frames fitted with thin unwired foundation can be used, and the comb cut into pound (454 g) squares and wrapped in waxed paper or cellophane.

Selling and storing honey

One matter that may take up a fair amount of time during winter, if the crop has been a good one, is the work of putting it into attractive form for disposal. Even the owner of only one or two hives may quite well have a hundredweight (51 kg) of honey which he cannot consume at home, and should know how to market it satisfactorily.

Whenever it is possible, honey should be put in the final containers immediately after extraction. The less it is handled the better, for every time it is poured from one vessel to another some of the delicate essence is given off, especially because, after a time, it sets solid and cannot be transferred without being heated—a process that accelerates the loss of aroma and flavour.

Bulk disposal Those who do not want to undertake retail marketing can dispose of their surplus in bulk to various firms who repack it for retail sale. All that is necessary is to run the honey from the settling tank into tins sold for the purpose. These hold 7, 14, 28 or 56 lb (3, 6, 12·7, or 25 kg), but by far the most useful, and the most easily obtainable, package is the 28 lb (12·7 kg). Plastic bucket containers of 2 gallon (9 litres), 3 gallon (13·5 litres) and 5 gallon (22·5 litres) capacity are also available for bulk storage.

Jars Many people will be able to find an appreciative market in the neighbourhood for honey in jars, so a certain amount, if not all the crop, will need packing in this way. Suitable jars are obtainable from your appliance dealer or from local bee-keepers' associations.

For convenience in filling, the settling tank should be raised on a bench, at which one can sit comfortably, with room for both empty and full jars.

Jars are filled very quickly at the valve and must be constantly watched to avoid running over. They should be filled a little above the ring which marks the correct height and the caps put on lightly at first. They should stand in a fairly warm place for twenty-four hours to permit any scum to rise. This can then be removed with a spoon together with any excess honey above the ring. By the time all jars are done there will probably be one or two more filled with this excess and after standing a while, they can be treated like the others. This extra care is well worthwhile, as it ensures even filling and the honey sets without a crust on top.

As the jars are completed, the caps should be screwed down tightly and a label put on. There is a large variety of labels on the market, and the bee-keepers' associations also usually supply one to their members.

Storing Although the jars are as near airtight as possible, it is wise to store them in a dry place where the temperature does not fluctuate too much. Nothing is better than a cupboard in the kitchen.

Sooner or later, the honey will crystallize in the jars, the time depending on the kind of honey. Fruit blossom and clover honey are rather slow to crystallize, while that from charlock and other crucifers sets so quickly that it is often difficult to deal with without warming it.

Naturally, granulated honey often shows what are called 'frost marks' on the side of the jar. They are caused merely by contraction during crystallization, and have not the least effect on the quality of the honey.

To produce a softer crystallized honey, the honey should be drawn off into tins and allowed to set. It is then partly re-liquefied by standing the tin in hot water, and then bottled. It need not be entirely liquefied, but softened sufficiently to permit it to be stirred until it is smooth and creamy and can be poured into jars. It will not set hard again, but will be easy to take out with a spoon.

If you have too much honey to bottle at once, it must not be left in the settling tank to set, but run into tins if it can be melted slowly at a moderate temperature. In no case should it be allowed to go beyond $140\,°F$ ($60\,°C$).

Care expended on packing and labelling jars or sections will always be worthwhile, as it will secure favourable notice at sight and a good reputation for the product, not only among consumers, but—what is more important when there is a good deal to dispose of—among the retail shopkeepers. The standard of packing of all kinds of food has reached such a high level that no shopkeeper will display anything slovenly or dirty in appearance, however good the contained article may be.

8 Beeswax

Beeswax is produced by glands under the abdomen. When gorged with honey and without comb to receive it, the workers cluster closely together, raising the temperature to the region of 90 °F (32 °C). Within twenty-four hours wax scales begin to form. They are almost transparent and roughly pentagonal in shape. They can often be found on the floor of a hive where they have been dropped during the work of comb building and look like small flakes of mica. The workers pick them from the pockets with the spines on the second pair of legs and transfer them to the jaws, where they are masticated with saliva, which makes them plastic. They are then stuck to the roof of the chamber or on the edge of a cell already started and so built up into irregular masses, which in turn are scooped out and thinned down until the familiar cells begin to take shape.

When built during a good flow the comb is usually white, but the shade depends somewhat on the colour of the nectar and pollen from which it is derived. If sainfoin is the predominant blossom, the comb is deep yellow, while that from heather is snowy white. In light nectar-flows new comb is often darker, because some wax from old comb is mixed with it. As the work proceeds the comb is coloured more or less by the addition of varnish, made from the resinous propolis which the bees collect.

Maintaining a supply of comb

The aim of the bee-keeper should be to have hives always furnished with the best comb, to retain it as long as possible, consistent with efficiency, and to prevent the formation of 'burr' and 'brace' comb by correct spacing. In spite of all care there will always be a percentage of wax wasted in various ways. In course of time combs become inferior for various reasons, like change to drone comb, injury by wax moth, or clogging with old dried-up pollen. The largest production of wax is from the cappings removed before honey is extracted, and this also provides the best quality.

The amount of wax collected in these ways varies a good deal. If the bee-keeper aims mainly at section production, his wax harvest will be comparatively small, but if he works for extracted honey, the cappings will amount to a considerable quantity; about 2 lb (1 kg) of wax for every 100 lb (45 kg) of honey. By the adoption of simple methods of collection and rendering the trouble is reduced to a minimum and some addition to the income is made. It is impossible to avoid the work of removing burr comb from hives, frames and sections, or to extract honey without uncapping and it is no trouble to store the waste in an airproof receptacle. Care should be taken to keep out as much propolis as possible, for the more this is mixed with wax, the darker will be the colour. In cleaning sections, for instance, burr comb should be cut off and kept as should the scrapings of propolis. Cappings should always be kept separate.

Rendering wax

The solar extractor   There are several ways of rendering wax, but the best appliance is undoubtedly the solar extractor, for this not only works without attention or fuel but disposes of the wax waste at once and thus avoids the risk of wax moth attacking the store.

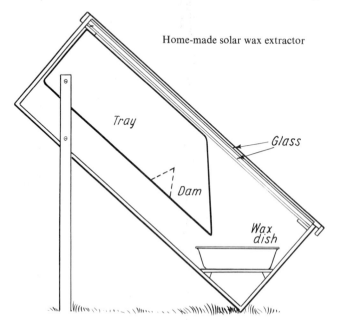

Home-made solar wax extractor

The appliance can be purchased, but it is easily made at home (see the diagram on page 56). It should stand in the open all summer, facing south. The waste wax is put into the tray and without further attention runs into the dish. From time to time, the rubbish in the tray should be cleared out while still warm. This 'slum gum' should not be thrown away, but allowed to harden. If broken in pieces about the size of a golf ball, it will burn long and fiercely, and forms an excellent pleasant-smelling fire-lighter.

Other methods Wax may also be melted in water, the method being to pack the comb into a muslin bag, tie it securely and put it in a pan or copper of water, with a weight on it to keep it down. The water is boiled to extract the wax, which floats to the surface and can be removed in a cake when cool. It is essential to use rain water, because any trace of lime will spoil the texture of the wax, but a little vinegar added to hard water will counteract this.

However, this method tends to discolour the wax owing to the resins and other substances boiled with it and it is better to use a steam extractor, several patterns of which are on the market.

Cappings

Cappings produce the best wax. The manner in which they are dealt with depends on the size of the apiary. Large bee-keepers usually have an uncapping appliance that automatically melts and

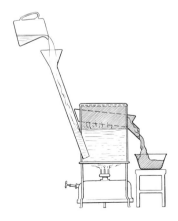

Wax extractor: water pressure forces the melted wax through the strainer

separates the wax. The cappings fall onto a sloping tray, which is heated beneath by hot water, steam or electricity, so that the honey runs off and the melted wax follows. In the more costly types, the wax runs into a separate receptacle, but in the cheaper kinds it forms a cake on top of the honey.

Those who do not have much to spend on appliances have two alternative methods of dealing with cappings. After they have been well drained in the straining tank, they may be put in a pan of tepid water, soaked for twenty-four hours and drained off again. Then the wax can be dried off and put into the solar extractor.

Another method is to use the cappings' cleaner. This consists of a box with metal bottom, supporting a tray of wire netting, $\frac{1}{2}$ in (1·3 cm) mesh, into which the wet cappings are placed. The box is put on the hive like a super and the bees enter from openings beneath. In a few days they clean out all the honey, leaving the wax as a dry powder.

Cappings wax is much lighter in colour than that from mixed waste, and all gum should be cleared from the solar extractor before it is put into the tray; it is the best material from which to prepare wax for exhibition or pharmaceutical purposes.

Foundation

Having procured the cakes of wax, either by solar or water extraction, the simplest plan is to send them to the appliance dealer to be made into foundation, but apart from any monetary profit, it is interesting to work up beeswax into various forms. It is possible to make foundation at home. Metal moulds for producing single sheets of foundation may now be obtained from the appliance manufacturers. Most of these are made abroad and are costly for the individual to purchase, but are quite within the capabilities of many bee-keeping associations.

Moulding wax

For retail purposes, wax should be moulded into cakes of 1, 2, 4 or 8 oz (28, 56, 113 or 227 g). Suitable moulds of metal or wood can be had from the dealers, but small glass pots serve well. An egg cup, for instance, makes an ounce (28 g) cake appropriately shaped like a skep.

To melt the wax, the only safe way is to use a water bath. Special double vessels are sold for the purpose, but it suffices to use a deep tin or jar. Break the cakes into small pieces, put them in the tin, stand this in a pan of hot water and boil. As the wax melts, more can be added until the jar is full. Meanwhile the moulds should be prepared. They must be quite clean but need not be greased, though sticking is less likely if a little olive oil is rubbed over the inside. It is important to have the moulds warm or the cakes may crack on cooling. There is no better plan than to stand them in a pan of hot water, so that cooling is gradual.

When ready, lift the pot of wax from the water and wipe the outside to prevent drops of water falling into the mould and causing pits in the cake. Pour the wax slowly and evenly to avoid air bubbles, but if any appear on the surface they should be broken while the wax is still liquid. When a crust has formed over the cake, more warm water should be poured into the pan, until it flows over the mould and the wax is quite covered. When cold the cake will float out of the mould.

Exhibition wax

The quality of wax at honey shows has risen greatly during the last few years and the standard must be very good to win prizes. Purity, colour, texture, aroma and perfect moulding are the requirements, and great care and attention are needed to form a perfect cake of wax.

Those who intend to exhibit should set aside all pieces from the whitest comb. Heather cappings are the best and, at large shows, wax from these has a class to itself. Apart from using special care to eliminate propolis, which gives the wax a resinous odour, carefully read the schedule of the show you intend to enter, which will set out the size, shape and weight of the cakes required. It must be remembered that too much bleaching and refining will spoil the aroma.

Those with artistic leanings will often take delight in moulding wax into fancy shapes; candles are now encouraged in competitive wax classes, and they form an attractive addition to composite displays of bee produce.

9 Autumn Work

When the harvest has been removed, the bees should be examined without undue delay, so that anything necessary may be done to get them into good condition for winter.

Very often, after the supers have been removed, there is no brood in the hive. If this is found to be the case, the first thing is to make sure there is a queen. If one is not found, steps must be taken to provide one, if the colony is otherwise strong. The most usual way to make good loss of queens at this time is to unite the stock to a nucleus. Otherwise a queen must be purchased.

If the stock has a queen, she must be induced to begin laying again. Remove one of the empty combs—this is an occasion when damaged, irregular combs, or those having too many drone cells, can be culled. This makes room for a frame of foundation, which should be put in the centre. Queens always prefer to lay in a new comb and this frame should be filled with eggs as fast as the comb is built out. It is essential to feed the bees, so a jar or tin of syrup is put over the feedhole, which will be immediately above the new frame. In a week's time the stock should be inspected to make sure that laying has begun. Steady feeding for a month or five weeks will generally ensure the raising of a good batch of young bees, the first essential to successful wintering of the colony.

The brood-chamber

It may be, especially after a particularly good nectar season, that the brood-chamber is full of honey, so that there is no room for the queen to lay; if this happens one of the sealed combs should again be removed and a frame of foundation put in the middle. In this case it will not be necessary to feed, since the bees will make use of the stored honey in addition to that which is coming in. The removed comb of food can be given back later on to make up for what has been used. Now and again it will be found that the queen of a prolific strain, like Italians, has filled the chamber with brood, while all the honey has gone into the supers. Providing the weather is reasonably good during August, nothing need be done for the moment, for the bees will be able to get sufficient for daily maintenance and the brood will steadily emerge and add to the foraging force. Special care must be taken to give such a stock an ample supply of syrup before winter and, if an abundant crop has been taken, it is provident to reserve a full super of honey to put over the brood-chamber for winter.

Feeding bees

It is true that bees do not, like other domestic stock, need to be fed regularly, and because of this many beginners fail to realize that judicious feeding is one of the most important aids to profitable bee-keeping. Even in bad seasons, bees rarely fail to get enough to carry them through the winter, but as the bee-keeper wants honey for himself, they must either gather very much more than they need for winter, or something must be given them in lieu. It has been conclusively proved that the more food bees have in store in the autumn, the better progress they make in spring and consequently the more surplus they gather the next season.

From October to March food consumption in the hive is small and steady. It makes very little difference whether the winter be severe or mild; during those six months about 10–12 lb (4·5–5·4 kg) of food is consumed. After March food consumption increases rapidly, owing to accelerated breeding, and although in fair weather there is no lack of nectar in the fields, the foraging strength is not yet great enough to take full advantage of it.

If spring conditions are bad, restricting income while the queen is laying rapidly, the loss during April is great and a really bad patch of weather coming then may mean the death of the stock if it has not a large reserve. That is why all authorities agree that at least 30 lb (13·6 kg) of food should be in the hive at the end of September.

Autumn feeding Except in heather districts, feeding should begin in September and be completed as rapidly as possible, for the cooler the weather the more reluctant the bees are to take syrup. As soon as the surplus has been removed an estimate should be made of the amount of food needed by each colony. The simplest and surest test is to lift the hive from its stand. If this can be done easily, there is obviously little food, but if it is really heavy, all is well.

Methods of feeding   Bees may be fed in many ways, but the simplest and best plan is to feed over the cluster through the holes in the cover board. The rapid feeders supplied by appliance makers are round vessels holding about 5 lb (2 kg) of syrup. There are some patent feeders made to hold up to 20 lb (9 kg), but they are rather expensive and have no real advantage over the simple lever-lid tin or plastic pail pierced with holes. The holes must not be large enough to let the syrup run through quickly: from ten to twenty, made with a fine nail, will do. It will be necessary to put an empty super on to hold the feeder, so the tin should be wider than it is high. Most of the special feeders supplied have one big drawback: the bees have to come right out of the brood-chamber into the feeder, which they are naturally reluctant to do in cool weather, whereas the simple tin delivers the syrup right at the top of the cluster. To feed a small colony, like a nucleus, with a pound (454 g) or so of syrup, there is nothing better than an inverted glass jar or other container covered over with muslin.

When feeding bees, the following rules should be adhered to:

1 Feed only after sunset.
2 See that feeders are not accessible from outside.
3 Make sure the holes are not large enough to permit syrup to run down and out of the hive.
4 Contract the entrances of all but strong stocks.
5 Take great care not to spill syrup about the apiary.

Syrup, candy and pollen   Syrup for autumn feeding is made from 10 lb (4·5 kg) refined white sugar and 5 pints (2·8 litres) of water. Bring the water to the boil in a large pan, put in the sugar and stir until dissolved. Syrup of this strength can be stored safely in tins and used as required, so it can all be made at one time. The time taken by bees to store the syrup in their combs depends on the strength of the stock and the temperature, but in early September a strong colony should take it in a week or ten days.

To feed liberally and rapidly is the rule in autumn, so that the bees have time to store and seal the syrup before the winter. Late feeding may mean that the bees have unripened stores, which will ferment. Every writer on bee-keeping stresses the importance of this, but tons of bee candy continue to be sold, because the novice begins to worry whether his bees have enough food. Candy is solidified syrup, which will not ferment. Bee candy can be bought or made according to this recipe:

Put 6 lb (2·7 kg) refined sugar into a pint (0·5 litre) of boiling water and add a teaspoonful of cream of tartar. Boil up, stirring constantly until the sugar is melted. Simmer for ten minutes and then allow to cool to about 120 °F (49 °C). Stir the mixture until it thickens and pour into suitable boxes or shallow pots.

On a mild day—it is useless to do it in icy weather—uncover the feedhole and slide the box of candy into place.

Spring feeding is not necessary if a full supply has been given in autumn, but sometimes a little judicious stimulation will urge a colony to increase breeding. Syrup for this purpose is made rather thinner than for autumn feeding. Its exact strength does not matter, but 7 pints (4 litres) of water to 10 lb (4·5 kg) sugar is usually recommended. This strength is also right for nucleus stocks or colonies engaged in queen rearing. Sometimes, also, a period of poor weather in summer may be made profitable by giving bees frames of foundation and feeding to induce them to build them out. If fed liberally, a stock will draw such combs out evenly and fill them with syrup. When sealed they can be kept to supply autumn deficiencies, but care must be taken not to get them mixed with real honeycombs.

Bees require pollen as well as honey, but there is usually an abundance of natural pollen stored in the combs and any super combs containing much pollen should be given to the bees in autumn.

Robbing

After the nectar-flow ceases and until the weather becomes too cool for bees to go abroad, they try to raid other hives. Not only bees, but wasps persistently try to enter hives and only strong colonies are able to keep them out.

The bee-keeper must be prepared for this habit and not only take every care to reduce its effects to a minimum, but must himself avoid doing anything to start robbing. Honey or syrup spilt around the apiary is a cause of it and great care must be taken during feeding operations not to splash syrup about. Feeding should never be attempted until bees have ceased flying for the day and, if any syrup is spilt, it should be wiped up carefully or covered with dry earth. Above all, hive roofs must be carefully replaced after removal and no cracks should be left for bees and wasps to creep through; it is amazing how soon they can discover the smallest passable crevice.

While the nectar-flow is on, hives can be opened without fear of interference, but when there is little to be had in the flowers, an open hive will be quickly invaded. Only experience will teach the beginner when the flow is over, for it is impossible to forecast it or fix a date by the calendar.

Particular care must be taken of small nuclei and colonies below full strength. Strong ones mass a guard at the entrance, but weak ones must have the doorway reduced, so that only one bee can pass in or out at a time. If a hive is attacked, prompt steps must be taken to assist it. A piece of glass propped up before the reduced entrance is helpful, for robbers keep trying to get through it, while the rightful occupants go round the side. Perhaps the best of all plans is to stuff grass into the entrance and leave it till the evening. The home bees will have to cool their heels outside until flying has ceased, when they may be allowed to enter. Next day a watch must be kept in case the raiding is renewed.

Winter preparations

The real danger in winter is not cold but damp and bad ventilation. Bees, like animals, require oxygen and this can be obtained only when air can circulate freely in the hive.

A good method of ensuring ample ventilation in the hive is to have a wide and deep entrance at the bottom and the piece of glass usually laid over the feedhole in summer replaced by perforated zinc. By means of very thin strips of wood placed inside the corners, the roof should be raised sufficiently to permit air to circulate freely over the board.

Naturally, it is important that moisture should not enter the hive from without. Nothing could be worse than rain leaking through the roof, yet often insufficient care is taken to prevent it.

For the purpose of ventilation, the bottom entrance can scarcely be too big, but there are dangers to be avoided. Mice are prone to take up their abode in beehives if the entrance will admit them. They consume the comb to make room for a nest and even if they do not cause the death of the colony, they spoil valuable comb. They must be kept out and as they can creep through a small space, the most satisfactory plan is to open the entrance to its full extent and cover it with a piece of excluder zinc; through this nothing larger than a worker bee can pass, while plenty of space is left for air to enter.

If the apiary is in a garden, reasonably sheltered from high winds, no further precautions are needed for safe wintering, but in exposed places it is necessary to guard against the possibility of roofs blowing off or even the whole hive being blown over. If there is danger of the hive blowing over, a rope can be passed over the roof and attached to a peg in the ground; the other end should be fastened to a brick to allow for contraction.

These preparations for winter should be completed by the end of October, so that the bees can be left undisturbed till March.

If snow falls or seems imminent, the entrance to the hive should be shaded, because the intense light from snow-covered ground is reflected into the hive and tempts bees to fly. They seldom get back, but alight on the snow and perish. A board propped in front will avert this and also keep snow from blocking the entrance.

Above: a glass sheet over the hive's entrance will confuse robber bees
Above right: Langstroth hive prepared for winter with mouse guard covering the entrance and the roof securely weighted

10 Spring Management

After the long confinement of winter, the bee-keeper will look forward eagerly to seeing the bees on the wing again and perhaps be tempted by a fine day to open the hive and inspect it.

Such days occur as early as February, but that is much too soon to interfere. It is rarely necessary to open hives so early in the season. If the roof is removed and the hand laid on the centre of the cover, the amount of warmth will indicate whether breeding has begun and by lifting the hive from its stand, it is easy to tell whether there is enough food. If there is any doubt about this, feed by putting on a tin of syrup, wrapping it up so that too much heat does not escape. It is when breeding has well begun that most warmth is required.

Water

At all active times, except during a very heavy nectar-flow, bees collect much water, especially in spring when it is needed to dilute the winter stores of thick honey. They can be seen congregating in large numbers at the edge of streams and pools, sucking up water from the ground or leaves. In towns they often go to house drains where, perhaps, a dripping tap keeps a constant supply of moisture present. In a small apiary one or two jam jars can be inverted over a board with grooves scored in it, so that just enough water seeps out to keep the board moist. If placed in a sunny spot, the bees will soon take to it, especially if a little sugar is put in the first supply. Some use salt, which seems equally attractive. In a larger apiary a tub may be supported on a stand and a tiny hole bored at the bottom to allow a continual drip onto a board placed below. A bird bath filled with pebbles for the bees to stand on will also serve.

In districts where insecticidal sprays are in use a supply of fresh, unpolluted water will do much to cut losses.

Opening the hive

Unless it is suspected that something is wrong, April is quite soon enough to open hives; if you wait till the apple blossom is well out, it will be about time to make the first inspection. If the colony is full of bees, nicely compacted on the combs, it is not necessary even to take out a comb. By blowing a little smoke between the centre combs, it is easy to see whether there is brood and that is all that matters. If the colony covers eight combs or more, it should have another standard brood-chamber. If only six or seven are occupied, a shallow super will serve. Opinions differ as to whether this should be put above or below the other, and it does not make a great deal of difference, but in the natural way bees work upwards to where their stores are placed in winter and downwards in spring as brood increases, so that to put the new chamber underneath seems better. The drawback is that in order to see how it is progressing, the other has to be lifted. If possible, this addition should be of built-out combs, as foundation is not so fully worked on early in the year. It is always better to get combs built in the height of the season.

A practice at one time recommended was 'spreading brood' by putting a frame of foundation in the centre. It is doubtful if this increases the amount of brood produced and there is a danger that if the weather turns cool some will be chilled, owing to the inability of the bees to cover a larger area of the comb in spring.

Cleaning the hive

Before adding the new chamber, it is well to scrape off any brace comb built on the old combs—the work of a few minutes with the hive tool—and to clean the floor board. It is best to use a fresh spare board, lift the brood-chamber onto this and clean the old board thoroughly in readiness for another colony. If there is no spare board, the brood-chamber can stand on the upturned hive roof while the floor is cleaned.

If a colony at this time contains no more than five bee-covered combs, it should be examined comb by comb to make sure the queen is present and laying, and to satisfy yourself that the brood is healthy. For signs of disease the reader must refer to the chapter on that subject, but here it may be said that sealed brood, which is not quite even throughout but has jagged holes here and there, or cappings which have sunk, should be regarded with suspicion. If there are, say, two combs of healthy brood, the colony can be covered up and left to expand for a few weeks. Sometimes a rather backward lot in early spring will build up to good strength by the time the main flow arrives. Judicious feeding may stimulate this growth.

If there is only one stock, it must be built up as well as possible, for at this time of year nothing else can be done, but when there are several stocks, it is sometimes worthwhile to unite two together. Considerable discretion must be exercised in this matter and only experience will tell whether a particular lot is likely to build up well, whether it might usefully be added to another, or if it might not be better to destroy it. However small the colony may be, if it is compactly clustered, has brood proportionate to its size and is active, even though with few foragers, it is worth helping on by some encouragement. Empty comb should be removed, a division board put next to the cluster to reduce the space and a good supply of food should be given. Additional combs are given as the cluster expands.

If the colony is not merely weak in bees, but scattered about the combs inside the hive, and it is probable that there is something wrong, perhaps one of the less spectacular diseases like paralysis, then it is wiser to destroy such a lot forthwith.

Uniting stocks

It may be that a stock fairly strong in bees has no brood whatever. Search must then be made for the queen. Perhaps one is not found, or being found, is seen to be old, shrunken and frayed: it may be that there is brood, but only drone. In any of these cases it is wise to unite the stock to another, having first removed the old worn-out queen.

There are two recognized methods of uniting stocks, but for both the preliminaries are the same. They must first be brought together by stages, if they are more than 6 ft (2 m) from each other. Each is moved in the direction of the other a yard (1 m) every day. When they have thus been brought alongside each other, the old queen, if any, is removed. If both colonies are weak, the best plan is to remove all empty combs, so that the occupied ones can all be put in one brood-chamber. Space the combs of the queenright one far enough apart to allow a comb to go between each pair. Now dust both lots of bees with flour, not too thickly, but enough to make them clean themselves. Insert the combs of the queenless lot in the spaces left in the other, close them up together and cover up. Some recommend that the queen should be caged, lest the strange bees should attack her. It is important that a fine warm day be chosen for this operation.

68

In the other method, which is only suitable if both stocks are fairly strong, neither brood-chamber is disturbed, but one of them is covered with a sheet of newspaper, and the other put on top of this. In due time the bees eat their way through the paper and unite peaceably. After either method of uniting, remove the empty hive and place the full one midway between where the pair last stood.

Bee-keepers of considerable experience are often concerned on examining their bees in April, to find them weaker than when they first emerged from winter confinement, but if the facts are soberly considered, this is quite natural. From the time the colony enters its resting period in November, when the hive is, or should be, crammed with bees, the workers are not subjected to any strain or risk until the early flowers bloom. Older bees die off but there is not a very heavy loss of population in a healthy stock. When the first spring days bring snowdrops, crocuses and early blooming trees, the old bees begin to forage and the treacherous conditions of these early weeks take heavy toll of them. The queen will have begun laying, but the number of bees maturing is small and quite insufficient to replace losses. Hence it often happens that 'spring dwindling' is more serious when spring comes early than in years when hard weather continues into March. So long as there is a good queen, this need cause no alarm; all will be well when the batches of brood mature into adults.

Strong foraging force

The chief secret of bee management is to have the strongest possible force of foragers in the hive at the time the main nectar plants are in bloom. Left to themselves, bees build up their colonies on the flowers of spring, pass through the period of reproduction and then collect the stores that are to carry them through the rest of the year. There is really not a great deal the bee-keeper can do to accelerate this development. His part is to select the colonies that give the best results, provide them with the wax foundation which enables them to build comb rapidly at small cost of food consumption and to see that *at all times, there is plenty of food* in the hive. Any period of shortage inevitably means slowing down of breeding and general development. Seasons vary so much that it is not easy to estimate in advance just when a particular crop will bloom, and the conditions which obtain in one district are often quite inapplicable to another. Hence the golden rule is to 'keep all colonies strong at all times'.

11 Increasing your Colonies

At the present time, bees are not only expensive, but are so much in demand that to get any number of stocks, they would have to be obtained from varied sources and the beginner may receive very inferior bees. It is far better to exercise restraint and build up the apiary from healthy stock, acquiring at the same time more knowledge and skill in management. If it is desired to have a special strain or race, one or two stocks can be obtained from a reliable source and can be used to make increase to a modest extent.

Before making any attempt to increase stocks, empty hives and frames of foundation must be in readiness and, as the demand for bee-keeping material of all kinds is likely to outrun supply during the active season, it is well to look ahead and get what is likely to be required during the winter.

Making a nucleus

Although making a nucleus is a fairly simple matter, to do so without materially reducing the strength of the stock requires a little care. On the whole, it is most satisfactory to make only one from each strong stock, as this can be done without seriously affecting its prosperity. A poor colony, unlikely to build up to profit-making capacity, can, on the other hand, be de-queened and broken up to make two or more nuclei. If the aim is to make increase and sacrifice the potential honey crop, even a strong stock can be broken up into three.

Generally speaking, it is desirable that a nucleus should have three combs—one of brood and two well stored with food—but if well covered with bees, two are quite satisfactory. An abundance of food is essential to a nucleus, not only for the nourishment of its members, who are not able to forage adequately for themselves, but because the acceptance of queen cells or queens is much likelier if there is plenty of food. Nucleus hives can be purchased or made, either to hold a single nucleus up to four combs, or two or more separate nuclei separated by partitions, with separate covers and entrances on opposite ends or sides. An ordinary brood-chamber can thus be divided into four parts, each of which will hold a two-comb nucleus. Those at the side have an entrance made in the side wall, the two middle ones have theirs respectively in the front and back walls. The advantage of this is that, while quite separate from each other, they combine to maintain warmth.

The new queen—which will have been ordered in advance—will arrive in an introducing cage, with instructions for introducing her, but such a nucleus will usually accept any kind of queen twenty-four

Transferring selected combs from an established colony to form a nucleus

hours after it has been formed, without any special precautions.

If a queen is not obtained from outside, one must be raised. A nucleus is taken out of the stock, but this time it must contain the queen and, so long as the old colony has eggs, it may be trusted to raise a queen. If inspected after ten days, the cells will be found well advanced and all but one can be cut out.

Under reasonably good conditions the stock should not be much handicapped by making this nucleus, but store honey almost as if nothing had happened.

Nuclei made up from colonies that have been raising queens need only to be deprived of all but one sealed cell which, in due time, should produce a virgin queen without further attention, but certain precautions must be observed when introducing queen cells to strange nuclei. At least two days should elapse before a newly formed nucleus is given a strange queen cell. If it consists, as it should, of young bees it will usually accept the cell, but sometimes it will be treated as an intruder and torn down. The cell can be given at any time after sealing, but it is usual to wait till it is almost time for the queen to emerge. It is seven days after sealing before she is ready to do so and, towards the end of that time, the bees remove the wax from the tip of the cell, leaving only the tough cocoon spun by the larva. In this state a cell is said to be 'ripe' and within hours the virgin will make her exit by cutting a circular piece out of the cap.

Great care must be taken in removing a cell. The comb should never be shaken, but the bees brushed or smoked off it. A good margin, not less than half an inch (1·2 cm) wide, should be allowed and to be on the safe side, rather more left on top. Cells affixed to a bar are removed by slipping a knife under the wax used to secure them.

The cell should be put in at the top of the nucleus, the simplest plan being to lower it between two combs and put a drawing pin through the piece of comb at the cell's base, pushing the pin firmly into the frame.

All operations connected with queen rearing should be carried out as quickly as possible, avoiding exposure of larvæ or queen cells to cold wind or bright sun. During warm days there is not much risk, but if it is necessary to transfer cells on a cold day, each cell must be protected. A good plan is to put them all in a small box and keep this in the trouser pocket, taking each cell out as the nucleus is opened to receive it.

Raising your own queens

There have evolved techniques of queen rearing so varied that in one of the most comprehensive books on the subject, L. E. Snelgrove's *Queen Rearing*, no less than twenty-four different ways of raising queens are described. It would be unnecessary to give such a large number here, but these are the principles of queen rearing.

Queens should be:
1 Raised from the best stock.
2 From larvæ not more than thirty-six hours old, fed lavishly with royal jelly.
3 Raised when drones are available.

Importance of the drone   Since the quality of a stock of bees depends on both parents, the drone is an important factor in the propagation of bees with desirable traits, but it is, unfortunately, a difficult matter to control. Mating cannot be naturally accomplished except on the wing, so that we are obliged to permit our virgins to fly at will and cannot choose the partner with precision, as with other livestock.

Queen-breeding establishments are, as far as possible, set up in districts remote from other apiaries, but even these are by no means secure. Wild stocks often exist in unsuspected places and there have

Artificial queen cells affixed to bars provide one method of queen rearing

Above left: worker
Above right: queen

Left: drone

been instances of mismating by queens that were raised on an island several miles from the mainland. Allowing a queen a possible flight range of two miles and a drone rather more, four miles cannot be considered a safe distance between the queen's hive and that of the drone.

In spite of this, queen breeders, even in not unduly isolated places, generally manage to procure pure mating for most of their queens by first controlling the production of drones in their own apiaries. A stock carrying the desired qualities is specially encouraged to raise drones by giving it drone comb, which queens are always ready to fill in spring and early summer. Stocks not possessing the desired qualities are deprived of drones by destroying drone cells and trapping any drones which, nevertheless, reach maturity. This is done by attaching before the hive entrance a chamber with excluder zinc through which drones cannot pass, as its only exit. A cone-shaped entrance leads from the hive into this chamber, so that drones entering it can neither return to the hive nor reach the open.

Artificial insemination   About 1927, L. R. Watson (U.S.A.) devised an instrument for the artificial insemination of queens. This and the technique for using it have been greatly improved, so that it is now possible to control mating by this means, but its use is confined mainly to queen-rearing stations.

Queen introduction

The circumstances under which queens have to be introduced are varied. The most common is the formation of nuclei for increase of stocks and this rarely presents difficulty, mainly because the bees are young and not aggressive. Queenlessness from death is perhaps the next most common occasion; improvement of stock by introducing a queen of better pedigree comes next; and last, most difficult of all, is the requeening of a vicious stock, tiresome and dangerous to handle.

There are many ways of introducing queens and it would be beyond the scope of this book to deal with them all. I can only describe the more generally practised methods.

The easiest of all is to make a queenless nucleus and give the queen to it. Newly hatched virgins will also be accepted by such bees, but they do sometimes tear down queen cells and kill the occupant, so that it is better to give a queen cell in one of the tubular cages.

Once you have safely introduced a queen to a nucleus, the way is made much easier to re-queen a queenless stock, for as soon as the queen has settled down and begun to lay the nucleus can be united to the queenless stock.

It may be that one is not able to form a nucleus, as when a stock has been found without queen or brood, so that the queen must then be introduced directly, using an introduction cage.

One queen only The first and most essential thing is to make sure there is no queen in the stock when the new one is introduced. Most cases of failure by beginners are due to the fact that they thought the stock had no queen when in fact it had.

If, in the height of the breeding season, a thorough search fails to reveal either queen or eggs, there is little doubt that the colony has swarmed so it may be a month before the new queen begins to lay: she is young and active and the novice may not succeed in finding her, as she will dodge from comb to comb as each is exposed to the light. It is necessary when looking for queens to cause as little agitation as possible. To keep pouring smoke onto the combs drives the bees hither and thither and makes it very hard to find a queen running with them. During a good nectar-flow it is best to do without smoke; open the hive quietly and take out each comb smoothly and carefully. At other times one or two good puffs of smoke should be blown in and the hive left alone for a couple of minutes, so that the bees may gorge. They will then stay quietly on the combs.

A fairly reliable guide is the general behaviour of the bees. If they are clustered closely, especially towards the centre, there is good reason to think there is a queen and this can be confirmed by closely inspecting the cells in the centre of the middle combs. If these are empty and highly polished over a small area, there is almost certainly a queen on the point of laying. The hive should be closed up and inspected a week later.

If, on the other hand, the bees are loosely scattered about the comb and sharply resent interference, there is every reason to suspect queenlessness. If a comb of eggs is available, it can be put in the centre of the brood-nest and left for a week. If no queen cells are started, it is safe to conclude there is a queen. If queen cells have been begun, the stock is queenless. It may be allowed to raise its own queen if no other is available, otherwise the cells should be destroyed and a new queen introduced.

Introducing cage   To re-queen a stock the old queen must be found and removed. The new queen must be ordered in advance and will come in a special travelling cage, accompanied by instructions for using it. The cage almost universally employed for this is cut out of a solid block of wood. Three holes are bored in it big enough to accommodate the queen and her attendants, who occupy two compartments, while the third is filled with candy, which serves for food on the journey and as a medium of introduction. All three chambers communicate with each other and are covered with wire cloth. At each end of the block, holes are bored to communicate with the centre; that at one end is covered with wire put on after the bees were inserted; the hole at the other end is stuffed with candy, covered with a piece of paper.

When introducing a queen alone, it is essential that the bees to which she is being introduced should be able to feed her and groom her to some extent. The size of gauze to allow this has to be $\frac{1}{8}$ in (3 mm) mesh. It is in fact undesirable for these cages to be used for introduction because they may have been contaminated in the post.

The type of cage recommended by Dr Butler of Rothamsted is preferable for the actual introduction and these cages are available cheaply from the appliance manufacturers.

On receipt, the travelling cage containing the queen and her attendant workers should be placed on its side close to the open feedhole of the colony to which the queen is to be introduced. Do not remove the plugs from the ends of the cage, but leave the cage exposed to the bees for twenty-four to forty-eight hours. This 'conditioning' greatly improves the chances of successful introduction, especially of queens which have been caged for a week or more, as may happen with imported queens.

After the conditioning period the travelling cage should be taken indoors and it will then be necessary to separate the queen from the attendant workers and put her into the introducing cage immediately before this is put into the hive. The simplest way is to open the cage against a closed window: the queen will run onto the glass and can then either be picked up and put into the introducing cage or gently coaxed into it. When the queen is in the introducing cage the open end should be covered with a single thickness of newspaper held on with a rubber band. The cage with the queen—containing no bees or food—should be put into the hive between two brood-combs well covered with bees.

Finding the queen To find the queen is the most tiresome task when a vicious stock is to be dealt with. One way of doing it is to remove the stock a few yards from its stand. This can be done at night, the entrance being stuffed up with grass or rags for safety's sake. An empty hive containing combs with food, but *no brood*, is put on the old stand and the new queen in her cage is laid over the centre combs. Then the bees in the old stock can be released; numbers will soon return to their old stand and stay with the queen. A day or so later the old stock, which will now contain only young inoffensive bees, can be inspected and the old queen killed. This lot can then be rejoined to the other by the newspaper method.

Bees without combs, brood or queen will almost invariably accept a queen, fertile or virgin, during a nectar-flow, especially if they are confined in a box or hive. A queenless stock may thus be quickly re-queened by shaking three or four combs of bees into a box, shutting it up for four or five hours—allowing suitable ventilation— and then dropping the queen among them. They should be fed until the next day and then shaken out in front of the hive they came from. They and their new queen will enter peacefully.

The laying worker One of the most difficult problems connected with re-queening is the laying worker. After a stock has been queenless their presence is often noted. They are workers with their ovaries partly developed, so that they can lay a few eggs. Their brood can generally be recognized by the irregular manner of its distribution. A healthy queen puts her eggs in regular spirals, so that rows of eggs are followed by rows of larvæ in succession. Workers lay their eggs haphazard. Because workers cannot be mated their eggs are infertile, so that only drones result, though reared in worker cells. An old worn-out queen also produces this kind of brood, but still lays in a regular pattern.

As a stock with laying workers will not accept a queen in any form, nor raise one from eggs given to it, the best thing to do is to unite it to a strong one by the newspaper method.

12 Pests and Diseases

Loss of the colony

Starvation   In practice, many things tend to shorten the life of stocks. Most of them die during winter and two causes account for by far the larger number. The first is starvation. Colonies that have only secured a modest surplus during summer, or have had most of their gains removed, cannot get through the long nectarless period between October and April unless generously fed. Long experience has enabled bee-keepers to fix 30 lb (13·6 kg) as the amount needed to carry through a stock safely.

The indications of death from starvation are that no food is left in the cells and many of them contain bees that have died in a last attempt to get food.

Queenlessness   Queenlessness is the second most frequent cause of death, and although the stock maintains strength through winter, it soon dies out in spring as the old workers perish. Signs of death from queenlessness are absence of brood or only drone brood in worker cells.

Brood comb from a colony that died of starvation. The darker cells were once occupied by worker brood

Bad weather Adverse weather conditions account for a smaller amount of loss. Strong colonies in a sound, undisturbed hive are seldom affected by the coldest weather. Indeed cold is not so dangerous as damp, and a frequent cause of death is a leaky roof, which keeps the interior constantly wet. When colonies die from this, the bees are heaped on the floor and often covered with mould.

Precautions against disease

Bee diseases are divided into two groups: those which affect adult bees and those attacking the brood.

Even when a disease has been clearly diagnosed, treatment is not always easy. The principal difficulty is to achieve isolation. To remove them from the hive for treatment is impossible, since bees cannot live long away from the colony. Nor is the isolation of an affected hive very practicable. For these reasons, it seems likely that whatever may in future be discovered, preventive measures by good sanitation and the cultivation only of vigorous stock will continue to be the chief bulwarks against apiarian disease. All who breed bees should cultivate only healthy stock.

One of the consequences of the introduction of movable combs is a tendency to retain them in use for many years, whereas under the old system combs were renewed almost every year. Systematic renewal of combs should be practised by the simple plan of providing each brood-nest with at least two new frames of foundation immediately after the nectar-flow and removing those which are defective.

Hives should be subject to regular inspection and cleansing to prevent the accumulation of waste matter. Healthy bees always remove rubbish from the combs, but much waste matter remains on the floor.

The most dangerous disease spreader is the robber bee. All bees endeavour, when nectar is scarce, to raid stocks unable to defend themselves. Such stocks are those most likely to contain disease and this is the reason why the first colony to show serious disease is often the strongest in the apiary, for having overcome a weak stock, it carries home, not only its food, but the disease it contains. Do everything possible to prevent robbing by keeping all colonies up to full strength; reducing the entrances of weak stocks; and taking care when feeding not to spill syrup and never to feed until bees have ceased flying for the day.

Food is also very important. Artificial feeding is necessary in every apiary at times, but there is no surer means of introducing disease than by feeding with contaminated food. Foreign honey or honey from apiaries unknown to the bee-keeper should never be given to bees. Sugar feeding, though sometimes criticized as unnatural, is much safer than feeding with honey not gathered by the bees of the hive.

Water is also a source of possible contamination. It is difficult to prevent bees from drinking polluted water, but it is a help to provide a supply of clean water close to the hives.

Should the bee-keeper suspect that his colonies are behaving abnormally, with rapid loss of foragers, or quantities of dead bees near the hive (although of course some bees die every day), he should contact an officer of his local Association for advice. Some County Councils employ a bee-keeping adviser, while others rely on the established bee-keepers to assist and guide beginners. The bee-keeper should also be on the alert for the ill effects of the careless use of insecticides: a contaminated nectar or water source can rapidly reduce the number of foragers working from a colony or affect its brood.

Brief Guide to Diseases of Adult Honeybees

Disease	*Acarine*	*Nosema*	*Amoeba*	*Paralysis*
Cause	parasitic mite in respiratory system	spore forming micro-organism in the mid gut	cyst forming micro-organism in excretory system	either virus or unsuitable food
Symptoms	crawling bees near hive with mis-placed ('K') wings	excreta on combs; inability to fly; decline in colony strength	like nosema; usually a spring complaint	loss of strength in late spring; black and shiny bees ejected from hive, trying to return

Samples of bees with a suspected disease should be sent to the County Bee-keeping Officer where there is one, or to the Bee-keeping Specialist, the Ministry of Agriculture, Fisheries and Food, Agricultural Development and Advisory Service, Luddington, Stratford-upon-Avon, Warwickshire CV37 9SJ.

Guide to Honeybee Brood Diseases

Disease	American Foul Brood	European Foul Brood	Chalk Brood	Sac Brood
Cause	bacterial infection	bacterial infection	fungal infection	virus
Time of death	before pupation or shortly after; after cell is sealed	about four days after hatching from egg; before cell is sealed	after cell is sealed	after cell is sealed
Cappings	sunken, dark in colour often moist and perforated; observable at any time of the year	usually none, but if larvæ die after sealing the cappings are as for A.F.B.	may appear normal but may be perforated by bees or removed	variable, often removed by bees; may be dark and moist
Position of dead larvæ in cell	in lower angle and along length of cell. Best seen in tilted comb from above top-bar	can be twisted spirally or occupy any position; look melted or collapsed	normal	normal
Colour changes	light creamy-brown to dark coffee colour, later almost black	creamy-brown to dark brown, observable mid May to July	yellowish-white to chalky-white, may become greenish brown or black	pale yellow to dark brown
Consistency	always formless and slimy *with* ropiness	soft and tacky; formless but *not* ropy	hard and brittle, like mouldy pollen stores	soft and moist; difficult to remove from cell
Scales	hard, black and adherent, always in lower angle of cell (see by tilting comb)	brown in colour and easily re-moved; position variable	none	loose brown 'chinese slipper'
Treatment	according to the Foul Brood Disease of Bees Order 1967. *Consult your Bee Diseases Officer*		transfer colony to clean new combs	re-queen colony

There are other less common diseases of the brood including stone brood, addled brood and bald brood, as well as conditions caused by chilling during manipulations or in adverse weather conditions.

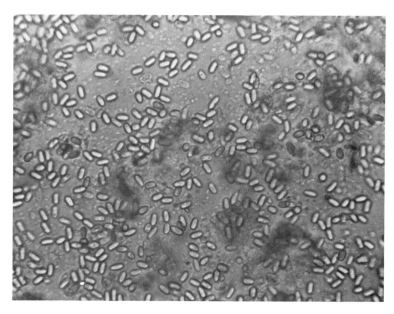

Above: Nosema spores
Below: Amoeba cysts in the Malphigian tubule

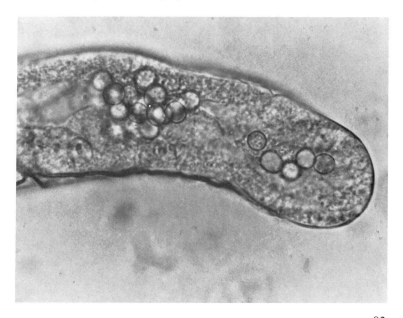

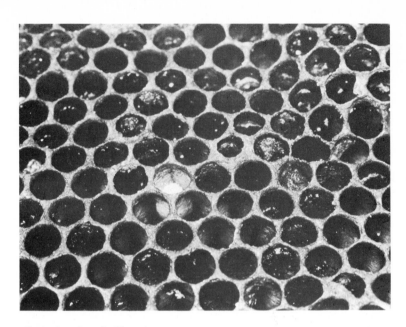

Above: American foul brood
Below: European foul brood

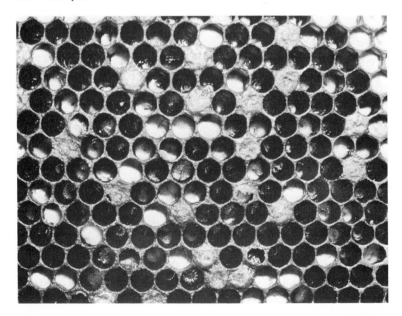

If there is any reason to suspect brood diseases, a complete comb, securely wrapped, should be sent to the Bee-keeping Specialist of the Ministry of Agriculture, Fisheries and Food, Agricultural Development and Advisory Service, at either Trawsgoed, Aberystwyth, Dyfed SY23 4HT (for compulsory samples), or at Luddington, Stratford-upon-Avon, Warwickshire CV37 9SJ (for voluntary samples).

Enemies of bees

It is only natural that a creature which collects large stores of honey should have enemies, for this is a food highly esteemed throughout the animal world. Against most of them the defence provided by nature—the sting—is adequate, but there are several enemies against which the bee can hold its own only by constant vigilance, and it is important that the bee-keeper should know what to do to assist in defence against these attacks.

Wasps Wasps, *Vesp* sp., are the commonest and most troublesome. Strong colonies can deal with wasps, for guards attack them on sight, but weaker stocks can soon be overcome, and the honey and brood carried away. The bee-keeper must keep his eyes open and assist such stocks by reducing the entrance to one bee-space. Care must also be taken not to spill honey or syrup about. Wasps have an uncanny knack of getting into hive roofs and taking syrup from the feeders so any back door into the hive will certainly be discovered by them.

Wax moths Several members of the family *Galleridæ* inhabit the nests of bees and two of them are entirely associated with the honey-bee. The largest is *Galleria mellonella L*, the greater wax moth. The small wax moth, *Achrœia grisella* Fab., is little more than half the size of the other species, but it is far more widespread and abundant. It is particularly troublesome in combs stored away from the hives. Many bee-keepers who have not inspected their spare combs for a season have been disgusted to find them reduced to skeletons. The simplest and safest method of destroying them is to pile the supers full of combs in a stack, paste paper round the joins between the boxes and put 1 oz (28 g) of paradichlorobenzene (P.D.B.) crystals on top of the pile, covering it over with sacks to keep in the fumes.

As this evaporates very slowly, it kills the larvæ as they hatch from the eggs.

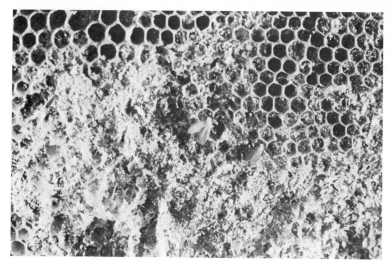

Wax-moth damage to comb

Mice Mice are also the cause of winter loss. If the entrance is large enough for them to creep through, they eat the comb and agitate the bees, and this causes them to consume food which cannot be replaced. There is no excuse for such an event, since a piece of excluder zinc tacked along the front will keep out mice and allow bees to pass freely.

Mouse nest between combs

86

Bee louse   This insect, misnamed the bee louse, *Braula coeca Nitz.*, is a wingless fly, parasitic on honey bees. Like all insects, these flies have four life stages. The eggs are laid on the cappings of comb and the larvæ tunnel along just under the surface, pupating in due course at the end of the tunnel. When mature, the perfect insect attaches itself to a bee, usually on the upper side of the thorax and lives by sucking honey from the tongue of its host. Queens infested with this louse may well be unable to get their full nourishment.

Apart from the damage to comb cappings, these creatures do not do much harm. They are very sensitive to tobacco smoke, which makes them let go their hold and drop to the floor. If they are found to be numerous, it is worth while to blow tobacco smoke into the hive, remove the floor immediately and clean it off with a flame gun.

Ants   Ants are fond of honey and bees do not seem to mind them. They crawl up the hive legs so it is difficult to keep them out, but standing the legs in tins of paraffin or creosote will prevent their entry. If the hives stand on rails, sacking soaked in oil can be wrapped round the legs.

Birds   Certain insect-eating birds, notably tits and flycatchers, take toll of bees. An effective plan against these birds is to push a bamboo cane into the ground on each side of the hive, projecting forward 45°. Between these canes fix black cotton in lines about 4 in (10 cm) apart.

In severe winters woodpeckers will attack hives, and can do considerable damage. Plastic sacking projecting from under the roof of the hive so as to flap in the wind will scare these birds off. A wire-netting case over the hive will also make entry difficult.

Badgers   In some districts it is not unknown for badgers to overturn hives and consume the contents. The only thing to do in such places is to make sure the hives are securely fenced in, remembering that badgers can dig under a fence not sunk into the ground.

Toads   Toads sometimes take up their stance near a hive and feed on bees falling to the ground, but perhaps they do as much good as harm by getting rid of sickly bees.

13 Honey Shows

It is natural that those engaged in the arts and crafts should take pride in their work and find it a joy to exhibit their best achievements to their fellows. In modern times this trait is fostered in public exhibitions of all kinds, and there is an annual round of agricultural and horticultural exhibitions all over Britain.

The bee-keeping fraternity is well to the fore in this sphere and one of the earliest activities of the British Bee-keepers' Association from its foundation in 1874 was the arrangement of exhibitions of bee produce. This society offers silver and bronze medals every year for competition at local shows. In addition to local shows, county shows are now very numerous.

The National Honey Show, now one of the most important of such exhibitions in the world, is held in October each year at Caxton Hall, Victoria, London. Over thirty cups, as well as numerous money prizes, are awarded at this show, which attracts entries from all over Britain as well as from overseas, and its schedule of classes can be regarded as a model for all such exhibitions. The show lasts three days, during which a programme of lectures and demonstrations is carried out. A large area is given over to trade and educational stands.

Exhibition qualities

Generally speaking, the production of honey, etc., for exhibition does not differ from the best methods of normal production, but for show purposes, the finest samples are chosen and special care taken to present them in the best possible manner.

Extracted honey usually comprises the larger number of exhibits, and is classified as light, medium and dark. This is done by reference to a standard colour glass of a specific tint.

Those whose crop comes from varied sources must make a selection of the combs before extracting. It is easy to see whether the honey is light or dark by holding the comb to the light. The light ones are then extracted first and the honey kept in a separate tin.

All combs chosen for show honey should be fully sealed, otherwise the next most important factor, density—or, more correctly, viscosity—will fall below standard. Any honey which is thin and runs freely after uncapping should be rejected for show purposes. It should stick to the knife, even though that tool has been properly warmed.

The selected tin of honey should be warmed by standing it in a vessel of hot water and then the honey run through a bag made of flannel, or alternatively through a nylon stocking into a clean vessel, in which it should stand a few days, so that any scum which rises to the surface can be skimmed off before the honey is bottled.

Containers

The squat jar of the pattern approved by the Ministry of Agriculture is now the standard container for shows. Highly plated lids are barred from some shows, but to ensure the best appearance the clearest jars, free from flaws and scratches, should be chosen.

Once the jars have been selected and well polished inside and out, the strained skimmed honey can be poured in right to the top and a temporary covering put on. The jars are then allowed to stand for a week in a warm place: a sunny window is very suitable. The honey at the top should then be taken off with a spoon down to the neck ring, and any trace of scum round the edges carefully wiped off before new clean caps are put on. The jars must be well polished and the labels provided by the show secretary affixed.

Granulated honey

Some shows distinguish between naturally crystallized honey and that in which some seeding and stirring has taken place to give a creamed honey. Only light or medium honey produces a satisfactory show honey in this class, as dark honey crystallizes to a brown muddy colour. It is rarely possible to produce a good sample without special treatment, for even though it granulates finely, there is nearly always a certain amount of 'frosting' which spoils the appearance. The granulated honey should first be prepared in the same way as for the liquid classes and then heated to a point between 140 and 150 °F (60–65 °C). While still warm, it is stirred steadily until it begins to thicken, when it should be poured *slowly* into the jars to avoid air bubbles. The jars should then stand in a warm place for a few days. Any scum should then be removed, after which the jars should be exposed to light until the honey sets white and firm.

Comb honey

Comb honey is exhibited in three forms: sections, cut comb and combs for extracting.

Sections The sections require careful preparation from the start. A full sheet of foundation is fitted with great care, so that it does not buckle, and each section should be quite square in the rack with dividers placed evenly between the rows.

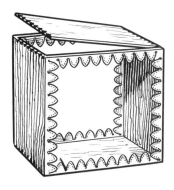

Show case for sections

Good sections can rarely be produced except by a strong stock in a good nectar-flow, so that all are quickly filled with one variety of honey only and sealed up rapidly. In hot weather a good stock will fill and cap over a whole section rack in a week or ten days. As soon as they are sealed over, the sections should be removed, for the bees will continue to add wax to the cappings and their journeys to and fro tend to soil the surface.

Special care must be taken in cleaning sections for show, and to facilitate the removal of propolis it is a good plan to coat the wood-work with paraffin wax before making up. Judges insist on being able to taste the honey, which they should do by opening one cell only and inserting a glass tube, so it is usual to put sections in special cases sold by the appliance dealers.

Show sections must be 16–17 oz (454–482 g) in weight, filled with

90

one kind of honey only, all cells sealed over with even capping, and translucent by transmitted light. There must be no popholes or pollen in them. Generally speaking, the whiter the comb, the higher it is classed, but the bright yellow of sainfoin is just as highly marked, other things being equal.

Cut comb   This is a recent addition at many shows, and is judged as for sections, except that the portions weigh about 8 oz (227 g) and lie flat in plastic containers. They also have cut edges.

Extracting combs   These may be of shallow or brood size—sometimes there is a separate class for each—and should be of virgin comb. They must be well filled, but not excessively bulgy, and the

Show case for shallow combs

comb surface should be flat and free from stains and markings. Cells with pollen in them are the chief thing to avoid. Special glazed cases are sold by the appliance dealers to hold show combs, but they can also be made at home by anyone handy with tools.

Beeswax

This must be in a plain cake, according to the weight range given in the schedule. Exhibitors usually have a glass case made to fit it, nicely lined to show off the colour, which may range from pale primrose yellow to deep gold. Heather wax is often given a separate class.

Mead

Mead is judged by flavour, brilliant appearance and attractive presentation. Plain clear glass bottles are usually stipulated for showing, as is a punted (indented) base.

Composite classes

These exhibits, sometimes called 'trophies', are generally a feature of the larger honey shows and, when well set up, they are very effective and add much to the attractiveness of the show. They are built up of sheets of plate glass, of diminishing sizes, supported on jars of honey and further embellished with attractive samples of honey in bottles, sections and cakes of wax. No restrictions are imposed on the size and shape of bottles, and often considerable trouble is taken to mould cakes of wax in delicate shapes. Little bottles of mead or vinegar can be added and some decorate the whole with flowers.

Miscellaneous exhibits

These comprise a wide variety of things associated with bee-keeping. Novelties in appliances or hives, cakes and sweets made with honey, photographs of bee life, oddities found in beehives, such as comb built in a peculiar manner, or the nests of some intruders like bumble bees and wasps.

14 Literature of Bee-keeping

Bee life
1968 Frisch, K. von *Bees: Their Vision, Chemical Senses and Language*
1974 Butler, C. G. *World of the Honeybee*
1974 Michener, C. D. *The Social Behaviour of the Bees*

Practical bee-keeping
1974 Taylor, R. *The How-to-do-it book of Beekeeping*
1975 Dadant and Sons *The Hive and the Honeybee*
1975 Root, A. I. *ABC and XYZ of Bee Culture*
1975 Waine, A. C. *Background to Beekeeping*
1975 Wedmore, E. B. *Manual of Bee-keeping*
1976 Hooper, T. *Guide to Bees and Honey*
1976 Mace, H. *The Complete Handbook of Bee-keeping*
1976 Vernon, F. *Beekeeping*
Min. of Agriculture *Beekeeping* (Bulletin No. 9)

Swarming
Min. of Agriculture *Swarming of Bees* (Bulletin No. 206)

Anatomy and physiology
1956 Snodgrass, R. E. *Anatomy of the Honeybee*
1977 Dade, H. A. *Anatomy and Dissection of the Honeybee*

Historical
1931 Fraser, H. M. *Bee-keeping in Antiquity*

Disease
Min. of Agriculture *Diseases of Bees* (Bulletin No. 100)

Queen and bee breeding
1968 Brother Adam *In Search of the Best Strains of Bees*
1969 Ruttner, F. *The Instrumental Insemination of the Queen Bee*
1975 Brother Adam *Bee-keeping at Buckfast Abbey*

Bees and plants
1974 Hodges, D. *Pollen Loads of the Honeybee*
1976 Pellett, F. C. *American Honey Plants*

Allied subjects
1973 Imms, A. D. *Insect Natural History*
1975 Crane, E. E. *Honey—a Comprehensive Survey*
1975 Taylor, R. *Beeswax Moulding and Candle Making*

Libraries

Many books can be obtained through the usual libraries, and many of the bee-keeping associations have libraries available to members. The most extensive bee-keeping libraries in Britain are the Library of the British Bee-keepers' Association, which includes the Cowan Memorial Library now in the charge of the Ministry of Agriculture in Whitehall Place, London, W1; the Moir Library of the Scottish Bee-keepers' Association at the Central Library, George IV Bridge, Edinburgh 1; and the Library of the International Bee Research Association, Hill House, Gerrards Cross, Bucks. SL9 0NR.

Bee-keeping fraternity

Almost every county in Great Britain now has a bee-keepers' association, with branches in each, and it will always be worth while for the bee-keeper to join. Addresses will be found in *The Year Book of the British Bee-keepers' Association*. The subscription is very moderate and the advantages derived from attendance at meetings, indoors in the winter and at various well-conducted apiaries in summer where practical demonstrations are given, will teach the novice a great deal.

There are many journals devoted to bee-keeping—for example, the *British Bee Journal, Bee Craft, Bee World, Gleanings in Bee Culture, Irish Bee-keeper* and *Scottish Bee-keeper*.

Those who are anxious to improve their methods and study the subject thoroughly can hardly do better than enter for the examinations of the British, Irish, Welsh or Scottish Bee-keepers' Associations, by following the course of study outlined in the schedule. They range from a simple certificate of proficiency in manipulation, to ability to lecture on an apicultural topic.

Index

Numbers in *italic* refer to illustrations